SPECTRUM

Geography

Grade 6

Published by
Frank Schaffer Publications®

Photo Credit: Courtesy of the University of Texas Libraries, The University of Texas at Austin: page 44; Courtesy of canalmuseum.com, public domain image of Panama Canal: page 56; Courtesy of the John F. Kennedy Presidential Library and Museum, public domain image of President Kennedy at the Berlin Wall: page 68

Frank Schaffer Publications®

Spectrum is an imprint of Frank Schaffer Publications.

Send all inquiries to:
Frank Schaffer Publications
8720 Orion Place
Columbus, Ohio 43240-2111

Spectrum Geography—grade 6

ISBN 0-7696-8726-1

4 5 6 HPS 11 10 09

Table of Contents

The Ancient World

Early European Civilizations

Asia, the Middle East, and Africa

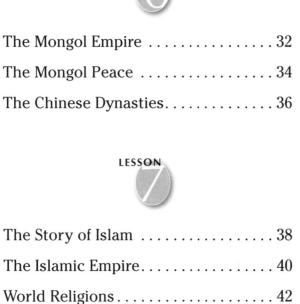

The Americas

Modern Europe and the Soviet Union

LESSON 11

LESSON 12

Issues in the World Today

LESSON 13

LESSON 14

LESSON 15

The Study of Early Human Beings

What does it mean to be a human being? Why do people act like they do? How are we connected to our ancient ancestors? These are just a few of the questions that some scientists ask today.

Archaeologists are scientists who study past human life based on items called **artifacts** that people leave behind. These artifacts may be items such as tools, fire hearths, arrowheads, pottery, or the remains of shelters.

Anthropologists study human beings and their ancestors. They examine artifacts and human bones, called **fossils,** to better understand past human societies. Determining the age of the artifacts and fossils they study allows scientists to tell how societies developed in different stages over time.

SOME IMPORTANT ARCHAEOLOGICAL SITES FOR EARLY HUMANS

Map 1

Anthropologists and archaeologists use scientific methods to determine the age of artifacts and fossils. One scientific method of doing this is a process called **radiocarbon dating.** Scientists also study **deoxyribonucleic acid (DNA)** from ancient fossils. DNA contains the genetic code for all human life.

Archaeologists set up a site grid at an excavation.

When archaeologists find a new area in which to dig, they first create a **site grid.** This grid of stakes and string works like a piece of graph paper in dividing up the **excavation,** or area where they dig. Using the site grid allows archaeologists to record every artifact that is found at the site and know the exact spot where it was found. It also allows them to keep track of the different levels in the earth where artifacts were found. This is important because artifacts at a higher level within the ground are usually more recent than those at a lower level.

Archaeologists and anthropologists use many different tools when digging for artifacts and fossils. These include shovels, trowels, wooden picks, and brushes. They sift soil through fine screens to find small bits of broken pottery or bone.

Each item that an archaeologist finds at a site tells something about the people who lived there. For example, the way that ancient people made their tools could explain something about their **technology** or level of knowledge. The bones of animals indicate the types of food eaten by ancient people. Plant remains such as seeds may also be a clue to their diet.

Scientists work hard to determine the environment, or climate, in which ancient people lived. They do this by studying samples of the soil and the remains of ancient plant life. For example, if ancient people lived during a time of plentiful rain and mild temperatures, this might have meant it was easy for them to grow crops. A time of drought might have forced them to move to a different area or find a new way of life.

The Migration of Early Human Beings

From the information they have gathered at archaeological sites, archaeologists have developed theories about how early human beings developed and populated Earth. A **theory** is an idea of how something may have happened. Scientists often change their theories as they discover new information.

Scientists think that early human beings, called ***Homo sapiens,*** first lived in central east Africa about 100,000 to 200,000 years ago. These were the first people that had a similar appearance to modern human beings.

About 100,000 years ago, *Homo sapiens* began to **migrate,** or move, throughout the rest of Africa and into southwest Asia. *Homo sapiens* then moved to Australia, Europe, and Siberia.

Scientists think that two other kinds of human beings lived at about the time *Homo sapiens* developed. They are called ***Homo erectus*** and ***Homo sapiens neanderthalensis*** **(Neanderthals).** These people also migrated out of Africa. However, *Neanderthals* eventually died out. *Homo erectus* may have eventually evolved (or changed over time) to become part of *Homo sapiens.*

Eventually *Homo sapiens* crossed a land bridge at Beringia, the point where Asia and North America met. From there, these people migrated throughout North and South America. This slow movement to populate the world took many thousands of years.

Map 2 shows the migration of *Homo sapiens* out of Africa into the rest of the world. Refer to the map to answer the following questions.

1. On which continent did *Homo sapiens* first develop?

In Africa

2. Which parts of North and South America were populated by water routes? Land routes?

_____

_____

_____

_____

3. Which region on the map was the first to be populated by *Homo sapiens* after they left Africa? Which was the last? Explain when *Homo sapiens* first migrated into these areas.

_____

_____

4. Use the compass rose to describe the migration range of *Homo erectus*.

_____

_____

5. Which regions on the map were home to *Homo sapiens neanderthalensis?*

_____

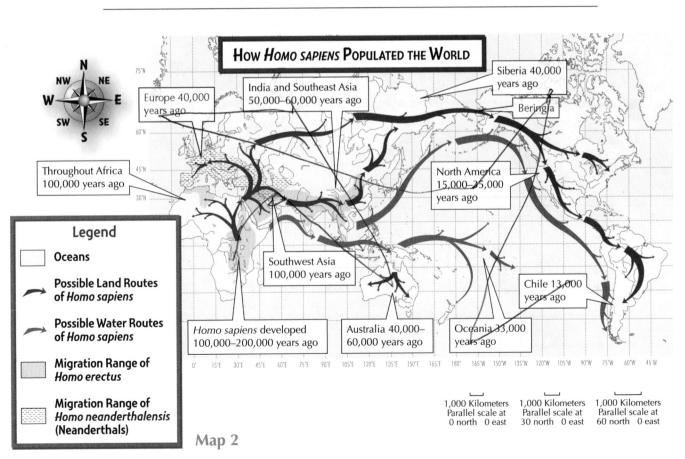

Map 2

More about Early Human Beings

Why is it important to learn about early human beings?

Use the information from pages 2–3 and the map on page 5 to answer questions 1–6. For question 7, you will need to do some library research on your own.

1. Use Map 2 on page 5 to create a timeline showing which continents were populated by *Homo sapiens* and when.

2. Name one important archaeological site of early human beings found in Africa, one in Asia, and one in Europe. Which of these do you suspect is the most recent site? Why?

_____

_____

_____

3. North and South America are separated by water from the other continents. How did *Homo sapiens* migrate to the Americas?

_____

_____

_____

_____

_____

_____

4. Name two other kinds of human beings that lived at about the same time that *Homo sapiens* began to develop. What happened to these groups?

_____

_____

_____

_____

_____

5. Why is it important for scientists to keep track of the different levels in the ground where artifacts at archaeological sites are found?

_____

_____

6. How can scientists determine the kinds of foods *Homo sapiens* ate?

_____

_____

7. Do some library research to form a theory about why *Homo sapiens* were able to be so successful. Write your ideas on the lines below. Provide evidence for your theory.

_____

_____

_____

_____

_____

Inside Earth

What creates a mountain or volcano? Why do earthquakes occur? **Geologists** are scientists who study Earth to answer questions like these. They develop theories that try to explain Earth's processes.

Geologists think Earth is composed of three basic parts. We live on top of Earth's **crust,** or outer shell, which is hard and very thin. Beneath the crust is the **mantle,** which is thick and hot and partly made of liquid rock. At the center of Earth is the core that consists of a hot liquid outer core and a solid inner core. (See Appendix page 96 for a diagram showing the inside of Earth.)

Geologists call the outer portion of the surface of Earth the **lithosphere.** The lithosphere is composed of the crust and part of the mantle. It is mostly solid rock. It varies in thickness from about 1 mile to over 100 miles. The lithosphere is not a continuous solid surface. Geologists believe that it is made up of many large, separate plates. These plates glide on top of a softer layer of Earth, called the **asthenosphere.** The asthenosphere is very hot, partly liquid rock.

These separate **tectonic plates** of the lithosphere move only a few inches every year. However, over millions of years, this adds up to many miles. For example, the Atlantic Ocean was created through the slow movement of tectonic plates away from one another over millions of years.

As the plates move, various things may happen. A plate may pull away from another plate; a plate may push underneath another; or two plates may just slide past one another. The edges of the plates are called **boundaries.** The table explains this in more detail.

Type of Boundary	Action and Result
Divergent Boundary	Plates pull away from one another. This creates new crust when magma (hot, liquid rock) comes to Earth's surface between the plates and cools. This is how the Atlantic Ocean was formed.
Convergent Boundary	One plate pushes underneath another. The result of this is called subduction. This destroys crust, driving it into a trench or pushing it upward to create mountains. This is how the Andes Mountains on the west coast of South America were formed.
Transform Boundary	Plates slide past one another. The San Andreas fault zone of California is an example of this.

Subduction occurs when one plate is forced underneath another. Within the ocean, large **trenches** are formed through subduction. Subduction also forms islands and mountain ranges as this contact between the plates forces great ridges upward over time. See the diagram.

Volcanoes may form along the boundaries where these shifting tectonic plates meet. **Volcanoes** are mountains where **magma** (hot, liquid rock) may erupt through Earth's surface. Earthquakes also result from the collision of tectonic plates. **Earthquakes** are a shaking of Earth due to the readjustment of Earth's surface because of plate movement.

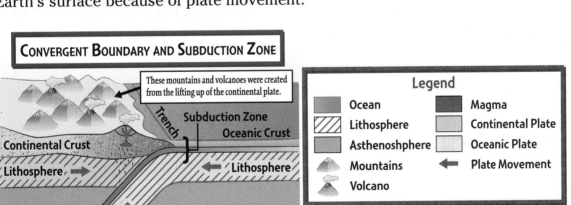

CONVERGENT BOUNDARY AND SUBDUCTION ZONE

These mountains and volcanoes were created from the lifting up of the continental plate.

Subduction Zone
Oceanic Crust
Trench
Continental Crust
Lithosphere
Lithosphere
Asthenosphere

Legend

Ocean	Magma
Lithosphere	Continental Plate
Asthenoshphere	Oceanic Plate
Mountains	Plate Movement
Volcano	

Diagram 1

SOURCE: Based on information from the U.S. Geological Survey

Build Your
Map Skills

The Ring of Fire

Geologists' theory of plate tectonics explains the location of volcanoes. Volcanoes tend to form along the boundaries of Earth's shifting plates: the edges of continents, undersea mountain ranges, or chains of islands. These types of volcanoes are called **plate-boundary volcanoes.**

Mt. St. Helens, Mt. Hood, and Mt. Rainier in the Cascade Range in the northwest United States are plate-boundary volcanoes. The Cascade volcanoes were formed by the Juan de Fuca plate being forced underneath the North American plate.

Some volcanoes are not located along plate boundaries. These are called **intra-plate volcanoes.** Geologists think that these form at a "hot spot" within a plate where magma is forced to Earth's surface. The Hawaiian Islands comprise a volcanic chain of islands with intra-plate volcanoes.

Magma is being forced to the surface of this volcano.

Many of the most active volcanoes in the world are in the Pacific Ocean area. Because so many are concentrated there, the area is often referred to as the *Ring of Fire*.

One of the deepest places in the ocean was made from the collision of two tectonic plates. This location is called *Challenger Deep* (see the map).

Refer to the map on the next page to answer the following questions.

1. Which tectonic plate does most of the United States sit on?

2. Which trench within the Ring of Fire lies farthest north? Which lies farthest west?

_____

_____

3. Describe the location of Challenger Deep. It lies near which trench?

Philippine trench. One of

_____

4. What underwater ridge has formed where the North and South American plates meet the African and Eurasian plates?

_____

5. Use the compass rose to help describe three of the plates that border the Pacific Plate along the Ring of Fire.

_____

_____

_____

_____

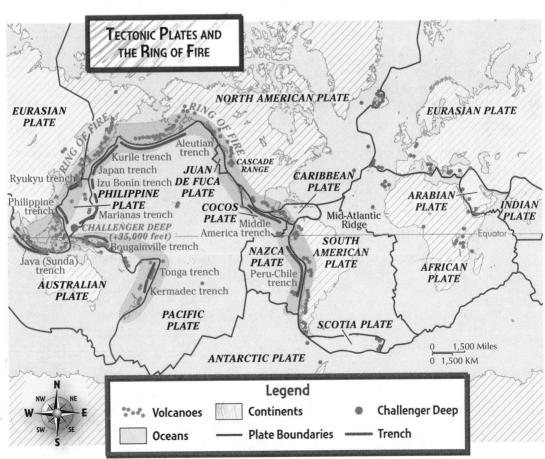

TECTONIC PLATES AND THE RING OF FIRE

NORTH AMERICAN PLATE

EURASIAN PLATE

EURASIAN PLATE

RING OF FIRE

Aleutian trench

Kurile trench

Japan trench

JUAN DE FUCA PLATE

CASCADE RANGE

CARIBBEAN PLATE

ARABIAN PLATE

INDIAN PLATE

Ryukyu trench

Izu Bonin trench

PHILIPPINE PLATE

COCOS PLATE

Mid-Atlantic Ridge

Philippine trench

Marianas trench

Middle America trench

Equator

CHALLENGER DEEP (+35,000 feet)

SOUTH AMERICAN PLATE

AFRICAN PLATE

Bougainville trench

NAZCA PLATE

Java (Sunda) trench

Tonga trench

Peru-Chile trench

AUSTRALIAN PLATE

Kermadec trench

PACIFIC PLATE

SCOTIA PLATE

0   1,500 Miles
0   1,500 KM

ANTARCTIC PLATE

NW N NE
W   E
SW S SE

Legend

Volcanoes   Continents   Challenger Deep

Oceans   Plate Boundaries   Trench

SOURCE: Based on information from the U.S. Geological Survey

Plates of Earth

Something to
Think
About

What great earthquakes have resulted from
the movement of Earth's plates?

Use the information and maps from pages 8–11 to answer the
following questions.

1. Which part of the United States do you think is the most likely to
    have earthquakes? Explain your answer.

    _____

    _____

    _____

    _____

2. Name and briefly describe the three basic parts of Earth.

    _____

    _____

    _____

    _____

3. What is the difference between the lithosphere and the
    asthenosphere? Tectonic plates are part of which of these layers?

    _____

    _____

    _____

    _____

    _____

4. When one tectonic plate pushes underneath another, what kind of boundary is formed? What is the action and result of this kind of boundary?

_____

_____

_____

_____

5. The 15 major tectonic plates are numbered on the map below. Study the map on page 11. Then, without looking back, match the numbers on the map below with the correct plate names.

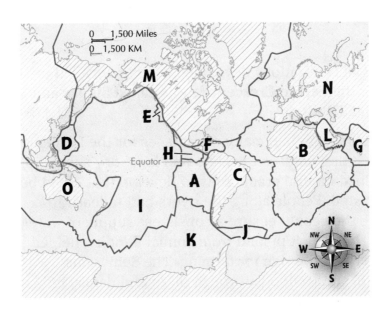

1.	Caribbean Plate
2.	Juan de Fuca Plate
3.	Eurasian Plate
4.	Indian Plate
5.	Arabian Plate
6.	African Plate
7.	Australian Plate
8.	Scotia Plate

9.	Antarctic Plate
10.	Nazca Plate
11.	North American Plate
12.	Pacific Plate
13.	South American Plate
14.	Philippine Plate
15.	Cocos Plate

Civilizations of the Fertile Crescent

The earliest of all civilizations developed in an area called **Mesopotamia,** or the **Fertile Crescent.** It was called **Sumer** and developed around 3500 B.C.

The Fertile Crescent had many advantages for the farmers who lived there. It had mild, wet winters and long, dry summers. The weather helped natural grain crops to develop that could be grown and harvested. People along the rivers had to learn to work together so they could ensure a consistent supply of water for their crops. The silt left behind from annual flooding helped make the river basin's soil rich for farming. The Sumerians learned to control annual floods through dikes and dams, and they learned to irrigate their fields.

These successful farmers created a surplus of food. Plentiful food encouraged the population to increase. The Sumerians also raised a variety of domesticated animals (animals adapted to live and breed in a tame condition), including goats, sheep, pigs, and cows. Agricultural surpluses provided enough food so that some workers could specialize in areas other than agriculture. Specialized craftsmen like jewelers, carpenters, and weavers soon worked for the ruling class. A strong ruling class imposed taxes and controlled workers. With its wealth, this ruling class built palaces and monuments.

Mesopotamia had little wood or stone for building or minerals to make metal. Sumerians had to trade for these things. Sumerian traders traveled as far as the Mediterranean and Arabian seas to trade grains, such as wheat or fish, and their fine metalwork for copper and wood.

Sumerian **city-states,** such as Ur, were independent of one another. Cities were surrounded by defensive walls. Within the cities were houses made of mud bricks. The upper class (including religious leaders and kings) had the most power. The rest of society consisted of nobles; artisans and craftsmen; free peasants, which were the the majority; and slaves. Sumerians believed that the kings were created by gods. The chief god was Anu, the sky god and god of all other gods. Other gods included Enlil, lord of storms, and Ishtar, the morning and evening star. Sumerians built temples, called **ziggurats,** for their gods and goddesses.

Sumerians were great inventors. They developed the first writing system, called **cuneiform,** which involved making marks on clay tablets that were then dried in the sun. They also developed the wagon wheel. They mixed copper and tin to create bronze, which they used for fine metalwork, tools, and weapons. Sumerians developed the plow, allowing them to farm large fields instead of small plots of land. Sumerians also made great achievements in math and astronomy.

Around 2340 B.C., a people from the north, called *Akkadians,* and their leader, Sargon, attacked and conquered the Sumerian city-states of Mesopotamia. Sargon created one of the first **empires,** or large area controlled by a single leader. Within a few hundred years, the Akkadian Empire fell apart. Then in 1792 B.C., Hammurabi from Babylon conquered Mesopotamia and created yet another new empire. Hammurabi collected a famous code of laws for his society, which became known as the *Code of Hammurabi.* This code of laws would influence many civilizations long after Hammurabi's death.

Sumerians built temples, called
ziggurats, **for their gods and goddesses.**

Build Your

A Map of Ancient Kingdoms

The map on the next page shows the region of the Fertile Crescent and some of the ancient cities and kingdoms that developed there. The region is also known for sites where early agriculture developed, and it was the location of the first literate societies. The Fertile Crescent is often called the *Cradle of Civilization*.

Study the map and answer the following questions.

1. What are the names of the two main rivers in the Fertile Crescent? Which general direction do these rivers flow? Into which large body of water do these rivers flow?

    _____

    _____

    _____

2. Name at least three modern countries that are located in the Fertile Crescent.

    _____

3. Which large body of water forms the western border of the Fertile Crescent?

    _____

4. What mountain range lies to the east of Babylon?

    _____

5. The Babylonian kingdom combined the territory of which two earlier civilizations?

    _____

6. A trading caravan leaves Katna bound for the Persian Gulf. Use the compass rose, map scale, and city names to describe the path of the journey.

_____

_____

_____

_____

_____

7. Name three cities that were probably important ports for shipping goods from Mesopotamia west across the Mediterranean Sea.

_____

8. Civilizations were slower to develop in regions immediately south of the Fertile Crescent. Based on the map, how do you explain this?

_____

_____

_____

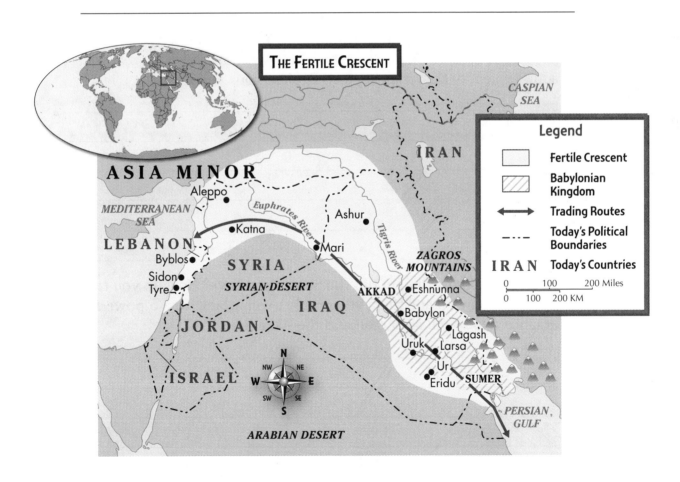

What Makes a Civilization?

Something to Think About

What is the most important thing about being a "citizen"?

In this activity, you will think a little more about the civilizations that emerged in the Fertile Crescent and what they can tell us about our own society today. To answer the questions, use the information on pages 14–15. You will also conduct some library research. In addition, refer to the information on Appendix pages 96–97 to help answer the questions.

1. Several Sumerian inventions are described on page 15. Do some research in the library to learn more about the Sumerians' accomplishments. Then, describe what you think was the greatest achievement of Sumerian society. Explain your answer.

_____

_____

_____

_____

_____

_____

2. What kind of government did the Sumerians have? How do you think this might have made them vulnerable to an attack from a powerful, organized foe such as Sargon and the Akkadians?

_____

_____

_____

_____

_____

3. What do you think are the three most important features or conditions needed for a civilization to develop? Explain your answer.

_____

_____

_____

_____

4. Of the features you named in question 3, which were present in ancient Sumer? What features does modern American society have that began in ancient Sumer?

_____

_____

_____

_____

_____

_____

_____

_____

_____

_____

5. Read the excerpts from the Code of Hammurabi on Appendix page 97. What topics do the codes address? What do they tell us about what the Babylonians considered important? Explain.

_____

_____

_____

_____

6. Do any of Hammurabi's codes seem unfair or unjust? Why do you think so? How would you compare them to today's laws?

_____

_____

_____

_____

Greek Civilization

Greece is a mountainous land. It is dotted with thousands of islands and has a long coastline with many natural harbors. The interior consists of small plains and many secluded valleys. Greece's geography influenced the way Greek civilization developed. The mountains isolated Greek cities and led them to become independent. The lack of farmland caused Greeks to colonize other areas of the Mediterranean. Their harbors helped them to become sailors and traders.

The first Greek civilization to develop was that of the Minoans on the island of Crete. It lasted from 2000 B.C. to about 1450 B.C. The Minoans were great sailors and became wealthy from the sea trade. However, much of their civilization was destroyed by earthquakes. By 1450 B.C., Mycenaeans were able to invade Crete.

The Mycenaeans were a warlike people who were also skilled sailors and traders. The poet Homer's great work, the *Iliad,* describes the 10-year war between the Mycenaean Greeks and the Trojans, who lived in present-day Turkey.

By 1100 B.C., enemy invaders had destroyed the Mycenaean civilization. Greek civilization entered a dark age from 1100 B.C. to 750 B.C. During this time, problems with farming reduced the Greek population. From 750 B.C. to 550 B.C., many Greeks left their homeland to colonize other areas on the Mediterranean and Black seas, seeking new trading opportunities and good farmland. These colonies encouraged trade with the Greek islands, which led to better times for the Greek people.

Mural, Palace of Minos, Knossos. The palace was rebuilt after being destroyed by an earthquake around 1700 B.C..

The 700s B.C. saw the development of powerful Greek city-states. The two greatest powers that arose at this time were Athens and Sparta.

Athens became known for its democratic ideals. The Athenian government, called the **polis,** consisted of an acropolis and an agora. The **acropolis** was a fortified hill. The **agora** was an open space that served as a market and a religious center and gathering place. Athenian citizens had the right to vote, hold political office, and serve in an **assembly,** which passed the laws. Athenian society encouraged the open debate of issues and the participation of citizens in government. Athens became devoted to philosophy and the arts. Some of the world's greatest philosophers, including Aristotle, Plato, and Socrates, came from Athenian society.

Sparta developed into a military state. It conquered neighboring lands and forced the captured people there, called **helots,** to work for them. Spartan society was devoted to strict military discipline. Young men between the ages of 20 and 30 lived in military barracks. At age 30, they could vote in the assembly.

The Spartan government was led by two military kings. A group of five men, called **ephors,** were elected annually to be in charge of education. The two kings and 28 citizens brought various issues forward to be voted upon by the all-male assembly. Sparta wanted to keep new ideas from challenging their institutions. To accomplish this, they became an isolated society. Spartan government restricted travel and incoming foreigners. It also discouraged the study of philosophy and the arts.

The acropolis in ancient Greece was a fortified hill.

Build Your

Map Skills

The Peloponnesian War

Athens and Sparta became great rivals. Sparta feared the success of Athens and its allies, called the **Delian League.** Sparta and its allies were called the **Peloponnesian League.** In 431 B.C., war broke out between the two rivals—a war that would last for 27 years. This struggle is called the **Peloponnesian War.**

Athens had become a great naval power. It needed a strong navy because it imported much of its food (most of its grain came from the lands surrounding the Black Sea). Sparta wanted to draw the Athenians into a direct battle with its superior army.

There were many battles in the long war. In 422 B.C., the Spartan victory at Amphipolis caused the two sides to reach a temporary peace. The peace gave each side time to strengthen its position.

By 412 B.C., Sparta had built its own strong navy with the help of its allies and the empire of Persia, a former enemy. Sparta won a decisive victory at the Hellespont in 405 B.C. when Lysander, a Spartan commander, managed to cut off Athens' access to the Black Sea and its important grain supply. This battle at Aegospotami resulted in a terrible defeat for the Athenian navy. The war then ended with a Spartan victory and a harsh peace for Athens.

The map shows some major events of the Peloponnesian War. Use the map to answer the following questions.

1. Use the compass rose to describe the location of Sparta in relation to Athens.

   _____

2. Name two city-states allied with Sparta and two allied with Athens.

   _____

   _____

3. Why do you think it was hard for Sparta to win a decisive victory without a strong navy?

_____

_____

_____

4. Name one battle fought in the territory of the Peloponnesian League and one fought in the territory of the Delian League. Give the dates for each battle.

_____

_____

_____

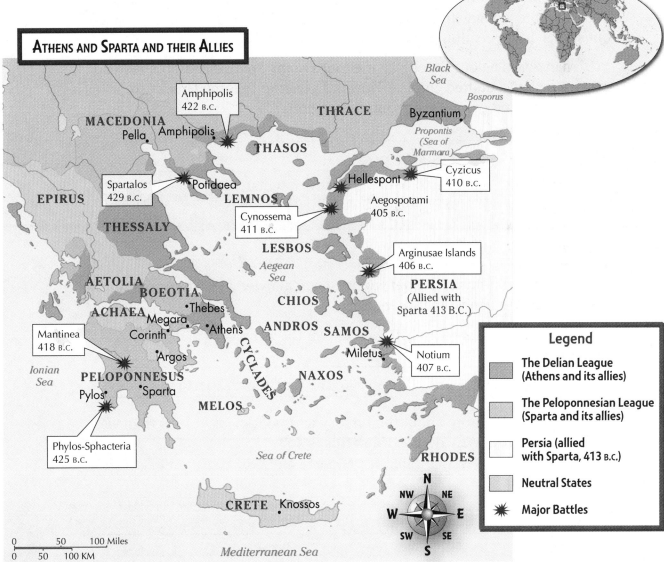

ATHENS AND SPARTA AND THEIR ALLIES

Black Sea

Bosporus

Amphipolis 422 B.C.

THRACE

Byzantium

MACEDONIA

Pella

Amphipolis

Propontis (Sea of Marmara)

THASOS

Cyzicus 410 B.C.

Hellespont

Spartalos 429 B.C.

Potidaea

EPIRUS

LEMNOS

Aegospotami 405 B.C.

THESSALY

Cynossema 411 B.C.

LESBOS

Aegean Sea

Arginusae Islands 406 B.C.

PERSIA (Allied with Sparta 413 B.C.)

AETOLIA

BOEOTIA

CHIOS

ACHAEA

Thebes

Megara

Corinth

Athens

ANDROS

SAMOS

Mantinea 418 B.C.

Miletus

Notium 407 B.C.

Argos

CYCLADES

Ionian Sea

PELOPONNESUS

NAXOS

Pylos

Sparta

MELOS

Phylos-Sphacteria 425 B.C.

Sea of Crete

RHODES

Legend

■ The Delian League (Athens and its allies)

■ The Peloponnesian League (Sparta and its allies)

□ Persia (allied with Sparta, 413 B.C.)

■ Neutral States

✹ Major Battles

N NE NW W E SW SE S

CRETE

Knossos

0   50   100 Miles
0   50   100 KM

Mediterranean Sea

Greek Culture

What are some important characteristics of American culture?

The table on the next page contrasts Spartan and Athenian cultures. Use the table along with material on pages 20–23 of this lesson to answer questions 1–4. Question 5 will require additional research.

1. Why was ancient Greece divided into many small city-states instead of a single, unified empire? How did geography force Greeks to expand and colonize surrounding regions?

_____

_____

_____

_____

_____

2. Why do you think Spartan women were allowed to own property while Athenian women were not?

_____

_____

_____

3. We know far more about the history and politics of Athens than we do of Sparta. Why do you think this is so?

_____

_____

_____

	Sparta	Athens
Type of government	Oligarchy (rule by a few)	Direct democracy
The "perfect" citizen	Disciplined, physically fit, simple, highly skilled in war	Trained in the arts and sciences; well-rounded and prepared for both peace and war
Lives of men	At age 20, tested on fitness, military ability, and leadership skills. Those who passed became citizens and soldiers. Those who failed could not become citizens. Military service ended at age 60, when soldiers could retire and live with their family.	Worked in the morning and exercised or became engaged in political meetings later in the day. Enjoyed physical activities, such as wrestling, hunting, and riding. Often discussed politics and philosophy at drinking parties (where no women were allowed).
Lives of women	Wives lived at home while their husbands lived in the barracks. They could own property and go where they wanted.	Very limited personal freedom. Could attend celebrations and religious festivals. Main task was to run the house and bear children. Had no political rights and could not own property.
Typical education	At age 7, boys were sent to barracks for military training. Cheating, stealing, and lying were encouraged but punished severely if discovered. Basic reading and writing taught but not emphasized. Girls also lived in barracks beginning at age 6 or 7 and trained in sports to stay fit.	At age 6 or 7, boys attended school, where they learned to read, write, and do arithmetic; they were also taught sports and music. Intellectual achievements were highly prized. At age 18, boys finished school and became citizens. Girls stayed home and learned household duties; few learned to read and write.

4. Do some library research to write a one-page paper on one of these topics:
   - The life and achievements of Pericles
   - Socrates' statement that "the unexamined life is not worth living"
   - Aristotle's Golden Mean
   - A summary of a famous Greek play, such as *Agamemnon, Antigone, The Trojan Women,* or *The Frogs,* along with a brief biography of the author
   - The standards for art and architecture of the Greek classical period (ideals of balance and harmony; ideal beauty; use of ideal proportions)

Birth of the Roman Empire

Italy is a long, mountainous peninsula that extends into the Mediterranean Sea. In the early days of the Roman republic, it had enough farmland to support a growing population. Also, the Apennine Mountains there did not separate developing communities as the more rugged mountains did in Greece.

Early Rome was engaged in war for almost 200 years in an attempt to control the Italian peninsula. By 267 B.C., Rome conquered its enemies and ruled all of Italy under the **Roman Confederation.** Conquered regions were granted self-rule. However, they were made into allies that would supply troops for the Roman army. People of conquered regions could even become citizens if they remained loyal to Rome.

Within Roman society, wealthy landowners were called **patricians;** smaller landowners, craftsmen, and traders were called **plebeians**. The Romans were distrustful of kings, so they created a **republic** (a form of government in which leaders are elected into power by the people). The Roman republic consisted of a powerful **senate** (with 300 patricians) and a number of people's assemblies. Two **consuls** ran the government and led the army. A **praetor** was in charge of the law that applied to Roman citizens. Rome developed a special code of law, called the **Law of Nations,** which applied to all people. The principles in this code of law would be adopted by many later civilizations.

Augustus was the first emperor of the Roman world.

By the 100s B.C., Rome was controlled by a small number of patricians. Small farmers suffered greatly from competition with this wealthy class. Many of them lost their land and were forced to move to the cities. This change was important because the army had always recruited soldiers from among the small landowners who believed in the republic. Some Roman reformers tried to make changes that would help small farmers, but these were resisted by the ruling class.

The Roman Colosseum was an amphitheater that could seat 50,000 people.

Powerful generals, such as Marius and Sulla, recruited soldiers by promising them land, but the soldiers became loyal to the generals instead of Rome itself. Generals became involved in a long series of power struggles, weakening the Roman republic. For over 50 years, Rome was engaged in civil war (a war fought between people of the same country) as various generals sought power.

Three powerful generals, Crassus, Julius Caesar, and Pompey, shared equal rule of Rome in 60 B.C. in the **First Triumvirate** (a *triumvirate* is a ruling group of three). But when Crassus was killed in battle in 53 B.C., the senate voted to keep Pompey alone in power and demanded that Caesar give up his command. Instead, Caesar marched on Rome, defeated Pompey, and gained control of the government. He became dictator, or absolute ruler. He was assassinated by a group of senators in 44 B.C.

Three new generals, Octavian, Antony, and Lepidus, then came to rule Rome in the **Second Triumvirate.** This arrangement soon fell into a power struggle between Octavian and Antony. Octavian defeated Antony at the Battle of Actium. In 27 B.C., Octavian, who became known as *Augustus,* was declared **imperator,** or chief commander, by the Roman senate. Augustus was the first emperor of the Roman world. This began the long tradition of a single, powerful military leader dominating Roman politics.

Build Your
Map Skills

The Roman Peace

The early Roman empire was mostly free from civil war during the period from about 27 B.C. to A.D. 180. This period was called the **Pax Romana** (Roman peace). During the *Pax Romana,* trade thrived, and the empire grew to its maximum extent. Though there were many wars and some rebellions in the provinces, Rome remained in control. During this period, there was a generally peaceful transition of power from one emperor to another because of the tradition of adopting a **successor,** or next person to rule.

The Romans allowed conquered people to keep their own customs. Roman citizenship was granted to many. This helped to maintain peace in conquered regions. The provinces adopted Roman law. The Roman language, Latin, was spoken in the west and Greek was spoken in the east. Cultural ties helped to unite conquered regions with Rome.

Emperors Nerva, Trajan, Hadrian, Antonius Pius, and Marcus Aurelius ruled during the *Pax Romana.* They were known as the "Five Good Emperors" because of their moderate rule.

The map shows how the Roman empire grew between A.D. 14 and A.D. 117. Refer to the map to answer the following questions.

1. Describe the areas that were added to the Roman empire after A.D. 14.

   _____

   _____

   _____

2. Name the major bodies of water that bordered the Roman empire.

   _____

   _____

3. Name one city in present-day Egypt and one city in present-day England that were once part of the Roman empire.

   _____

4. Use the compass rose and names of regions to describe two areas on the map that were not part of the Roman empire.

_____

_____and_____

_____

_____

5. Name two Roman provinces in present-day France, and name two Roman provinces in present-day Spain.

_____

_____

_____

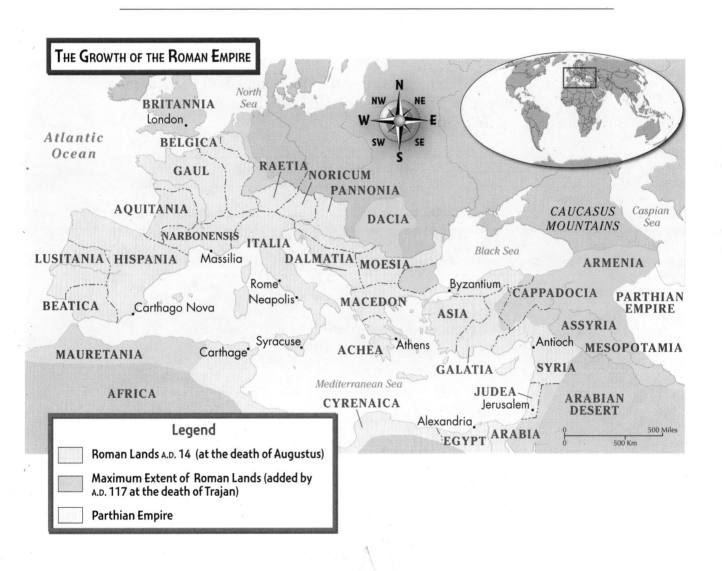

THE GROWTH OF THE ROMAN EMPIRE

Legend

Roman Lands A.D. 14 (at the death of Augustus)

Maximum Extent of Roman Lands (added by A.D. 117 at the death of Trajan)

Parthian Empire

The Culture of Rome

Something to Think About

What aspects of American culture will be remembered 2,000 years from now?

Use the material on pages 26–29 of this lesson to answer questions 1–4. Question 5 will require additional research.

1. Name one major difference between the development of early Rome and the development of early Greece. (Refer to Lesson 4, "Greek Civilization," if necessary.)

_____

_____

_____

_____

_____

_____

2. What was the difference between patricians and plebeians?

_____

_____

_____

_____

3. What is a republic?

_____

_____

_____

_____

4. Describe how Rome slowly changed from a republic to an empire ruled by one man.

_____

_____

_____

_____

_____

_____

_____

_____

_____

_____

_____

_____

_____

_____

_____

_____

5. Select one of the topics from the list below. Do some library research to write a two-page paper on one of the following topics. Feel free to add visual aids, drawings, or photos to your report.

- The principles of law from the Law of Nations and/or the Twelve Tables and their influence

- A brief biography about one of the "Five Good Emperors," focusing on his main accomplishments and failures

- The names and roles of the Roman gods and goddesses

- A summary of the plot of Virgil's _Aeneid_ or Ovid's _Metamorphoses_

- The role of women in Roman society

- A summary of the teachings of _Meditations,_ by Marcus Aurelius

- The characteristics of Roman art

- A list of problems that led to the fall of the Roman empire

- A summary of the Romulus and Remus story and what it tells about the Romans' sense of their own importance

The Mongol Empire

The Mongols were originally clans with separate kings from the Gobi Desert region of Mongolia. In 1206, they were unified by the leader Temujin, who was elected **Genghis Khan,** or *universal ruler.* Immediately, he began his campaigns of conquest.

Genghis Khan had a mobile army of superior horsemen. They fought from horseback, quickly striking their targets and inspiring terror in their enemies. Genghis Khan was merciless with conquered people. If they rebelled, he slaughtered them and destroyed their cities. By his death in 1227, Mongol armies had created one of the largest empires in history.

Following Genghis Khan's death, the empire was divided into four separate territories, or **khanates.** Each khanate was controlled by a son of Genghis Khan. The northern part of the empire extended from eastern Europe to Siberia; the southern part extended from the Arabian Peninsula to China.

In 1279, the Mongols completed the conquest of China that Genghis Khan had begun. China's Song Dynasty collapsed and **Kublai Khan,** a grandson of Genghis Khan, established the **Yuan,** or **Mongol Dynasty,** in its place. He ruled until 1294 from his capital Khanbaliq (present-day Beijing).

At first, the Yuan simply took the wealth of China. But because they wanted to build a strong government, they adapted to the Chinese government structure and practices. Generally, they allowed conquered people to keep their traditional ways. But the Yuan refused to learn Chinese. They did away with the Chinese civil service examinations for government jobs, and they kept the highest government positions for themselves.

The Yuan created a "four-class system" within China with themselves at the top. Next in order were their allies from central Asia (semu) and then the northern Chinese (han). The southern Chinese (nan) were at the bottom.

Kublai Khan was very interested in foreign cultures and religions. He invited people of all faiths to his court for lively discussions. From 1275 to 1291, the famous Italian traveler Marco Polo served as an official at his court. Marco Polo traveled for many years through Asia and returned to Europe to describe the wonders of Chinese and Asian civilization in his famous writings.

The Yuan Dynasty lasted only about 100 years. Other Mongols thought that the Yuan had become too Chinese, and they rebelled against them. At the same time, the Chinese saw the Yuan as an occupying army and never really accepted them as rulers. In 1368, Zhu Yuanzhang, a Chinese peasant, led a rebellion against the Yuan and drove them out of China. He then established the Ming Dynasty. Ming emperors put great effort into the reconstruction of China's Great Wall to the north to keep the Mongols out of their lands.

The Great Wall of China helped the Ming Dynasty protect China from Mongol invaders.

Build Your
Map Skills

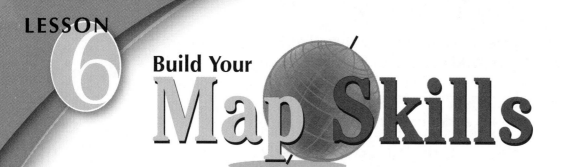

The Mongol Peace

As you already learned, the Mongol empire was eventually divided into four khanates. Each went to a son of Genghis Khan. The ruler of Mongolia and China, called the *Great Khanate,* was the overlord of the entire Mongol empire.

The Mongol empire connected the eastern world with the western world. Previously these cultures had been separated because of great geographical distances and the many separate kingdoms that made travel difficult. The phrase ***Pax Mongolica*** (Mongol Peace) was used to describe this period of strong and stable rule.

The Mongol rulers were generally tolerant of other religions and cultures. They encouraged trade by making east-west trade routes safe for travelers. These ancient trade routes, together called the **Silk Road,** were among the earliest connections between the cultures of Europe and Asia.

Use the map to answer the following questions.

1. Which khanate occupied the northwestern region of the Mongol empire? Which khanate occupied the southwestern region of the empire? Name a principal city in each region.

    _____

    _____

2. Describe the water route a trader would have followed when journeying from Rome to Hangzhou. Use the compass rose to help with your description.

    _____

    _____

    _____

    _____

    _____

    _____

3. Which geographical barrier might have made it difficult for the Mongols to advance south into India?

_____

4. Into which areas south of China did the Mongol empire advance after 1240?

_____

5. What geographical areas did the Great Wall separate?

_____

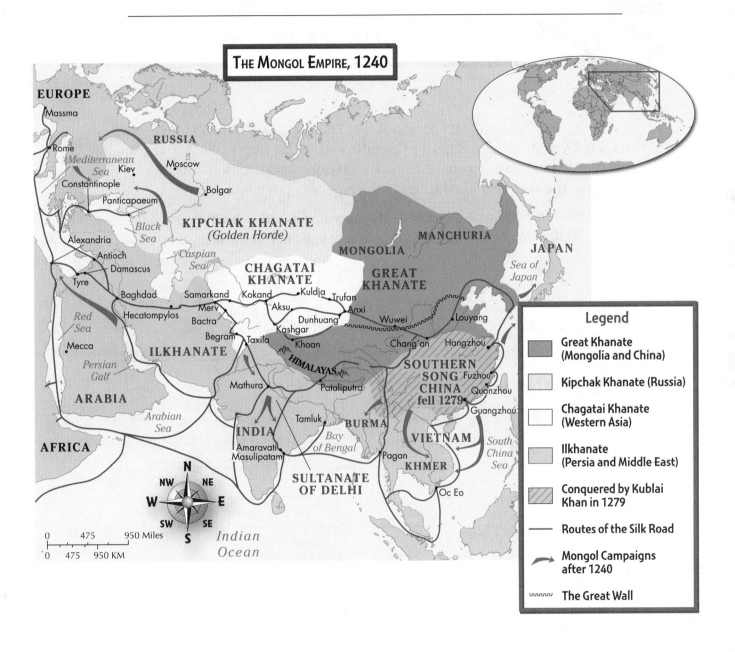

THE MONGOL EMPIRE, 1240

EUROPE
Massma
Rome
Mediterranean Sea
Kiev
Constantinople
Panticapaeum
Alexandria
Antioch
Damascus
Tyre
Baghdad
Hecatompylos
Mecca
Red Sea
Persian Gulf
ARABIA
Arabian Sea
AFRICA

RUSSIA
Moscow
Bolgar
KIPCHAK KHANATE
(Golden Horde)
Black Sea
Caspian Sea
CHAGATAI KHANATE
Samarkand
Merv
Bactra
Begram
ILKHANATE
Mathura
INDIA
Amaravati
Masulipatam
Kokand
Aksu
Kashgar
Taxila
Khoan
HIMALAYAS
Pataliputra
Tamluk
SULTANATE OF DELHI
Kuldja
Trufan
Dunhuang
Anxi
MONGOLIA
GREAT KHANATE
MANCHURIA
Wuwei
Chang'an
SOUTHERN SONG CHINA fell 1279
BURMA
Bay of Bengal
Pagan
VIETNAM
KHMER
Oc Eo
JAPAN
Sea of Japan
Louyang
Hangzhou
Fuzhou
Quanzhou
Guangzhou
South China Sea

Indian Ocean

N NW NE W E SW SE S

0   475   950 Miles
0   475   950 KM

Legend
Great Khanate (Mongolia and China)
Kipchak Khanate (Russia)
Chagatai Khanate (Western Asia)
Ilkhanate (Persia and Middle East)
Conquered by Kublai Khan in 1279
Routes of the Silk Road
Mongol Campaigns after 1240
The Great Wall

The Chinese Dynasties

What is the most important American accomplishment of the last 25 years?

In this lesson, you learned about the Yuan Dynasty in China and how the Ming Dynasty began. Refer to the information on pages 32–35 and the table on the next page to answer more questions about China and its dynasties. You will also need to refer to Appendix page 98.

1. Identify the first major Chinese dynasty and the dates when it flourished. What major accomplishments occurred during this period?

_____

_____

_____

_____

2. Which dynasty collapsed when the Mongols invaded China?

_____

3. In which dynasty did the building of the Great Wall begin? In which dynasties was the wall refortified? Why was the wall strengthened?

_____

_____

_____

4. Which of the inventions in the graph on the next page do you think was the most important? Why?

_____

_____

5. According to the graph, when was the iron plow invented in China, and when was it first used in the West? How much time passed from the time the iron plow was invented until it was used in the West?

_____

_____

6. During which dynasty was paper invented in China?

_____

7. When did Marco Polo visit China? Name two items in the graph he might have seen for the first time on his visit. How do you know?

_____

_____

_____

8. Use the information from your own library research to write three paragraphs on a separate piece of paper about which Chinese dynasty you think was the greatest or most important. Make sure to use specific examples to justify your argument.

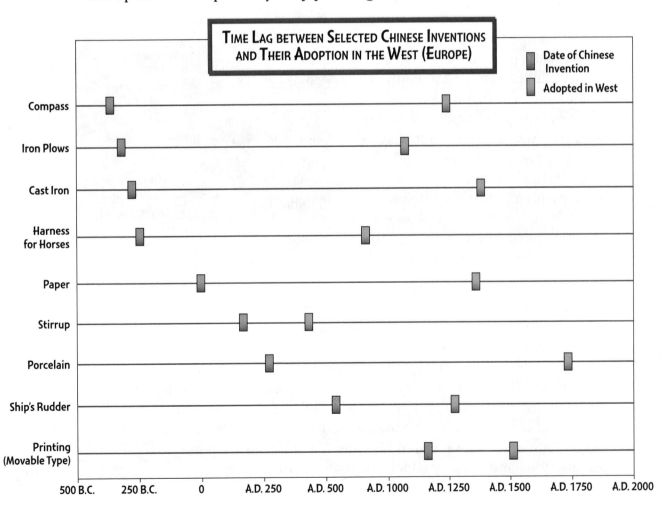

TIME LAG BETWEEN SELECTED CHINESE INVENTIONS AND THEIR ADOPTION IN THE WEST (EUROPE)

Date of Chinese Invention
Adopted in West

The Story of Islam

The Arabian Peninsula is a harsh land that is mostly desert. For centuries, the Arab people made a living mostly by farming and herding sheep. Many Arabs were nomadic. In other words, they were always on the move in search of pastures that would provide water and food for their livestock. Because there is very little rainfall in the Arabian Peninsula, there are no lakes or rivers. So cities grew up at oases, or locations that had adequate groundwater.

Caravan trade routes through the Arabian Peninsula became important to the economy there. (A caravan is a group traveling together, often with pack animals such as mules or camels.) The city of Mecca was an important oasis along one of these routes, and some people in this area became wealthy merchants because of the trade from caravans. Many Arabs also traveled to Mecca to worship at the **Kaaba,** a religious shrine.

The holy city of Mecca is the site of an important pilgrimage for Muslims.

The prophet Muhammad was born in A.D. 570 in the city of Mecca. There, he became known as an honest and successful merchant. However, he became concerned about the greed of the successful traders in Mecca and the corruption of society. Deeply dismayed, Muhammad often went to a cave at nearby Mount Hira to meditate. There, he received revelations from Allah, or God, through the archangel Gabriel. These revelations were written down and became the holy book called the **Quran.** The followers of the religion of **Islam,** called **Muslims,** look to this holy book for the rules and laws by which they should live.

At first, Muhammad was mistreated by the wealthy traders in Mecca, who did not believe that he was a prophet. So, in 622, he and some of his supporters moved to the city of Medina. This journey later became known as the **Hijrah.** (The year 622 became the first year in the Islamic calendar.) Eventually, Muhammad became a strong leader with many followers. In 630, he returned to Mecca with a large army. Most people in the city converted to Islam. Muhammad then made the Kaaba into a shrine of Islam. (This is why, at some point in their lives, all Muslims try to visit Mecca as a pilgrimage, or **hajj.**) A few years later, Muhammad died.

Muhammad taught that there is one god, Allah, who created the universe. The religion of Islam offers salvation and an afterlife. Muslims look to their code of law, called the **Shariah,** to guide their everyday lives. Laws in the Shariah deal with almost every aspect of Islamic life, including marriage, criminal acts, and even the economy. It is important for all Muslims to follow the **Five Pillars of Islam,** the foundation for Muslim life. The Five Pillars are methods of worship that are written in the Quran.

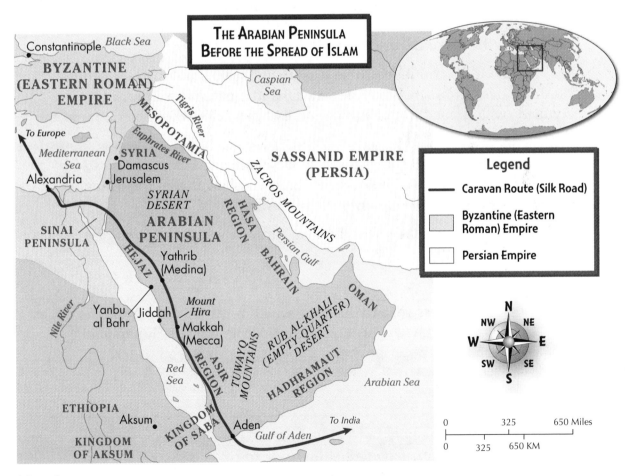

Map 1

Build Your Map Skills

The Islamic Empire

After his death, Muhammad's followers chose Abu Bakr to be caliph, or successor. Islam soon expanded into an empire under this new leadership, with Medina as the capital city. After the death of Abu Bakr, the next three caliphs were assassinated in power struggles.

In 661, Muawiyah became caliph and created the **Umayyad dynasty.** The Umayyads continued to expand Arab rule, but problems quickly developed. Many believed that the Umayyads were corrupt. Muhammad's grandson, Hussein, led a revolt against them. Hussein was soon killed in battle by the Umayyads, but his rebellion split Islam into two groups—the **Sunni** (loyal to the Umayyads) and the **Shiite** (loyal to Hussein). This split remains in the Muslim world today.

Many Arabs continued to be dissatisfied with Umayyad rule. Abu al-Abbas overthrew the Umayyads in 750 and created the **Abbasid dynasty,** which ruled from Baghdad until about 1258, when the city was sacked by invading Mongols.

Map 1 on page 39 shows the Arabian Peninsula before the spread of Islam. Map 2 on page 41 illustrates the spread of Islam and the Islamic empire. Use both maps to answer the following questions.

1. Name the cities shown on the map through which the Silk Road passed.

_____

2. Use the compass rose to describe which portion of the Arabian Peninsula was under Muslim rule during the time of Muhammad. Which body of water provided the empire's western border?

_____

_____

_____

_____

3. In which directions did the Islamic empire spread under the first four caliphs? Name three territories and three cities that came under Muslim rule during this time.

_____

_____

_____

_____

4. Name an area of Europe that was part of the Islamic empire.

_____

5. Name a part of Europe that Muslims invaded but did not conquer. What major battle was fought in that region and when was it fought?

_____

_____

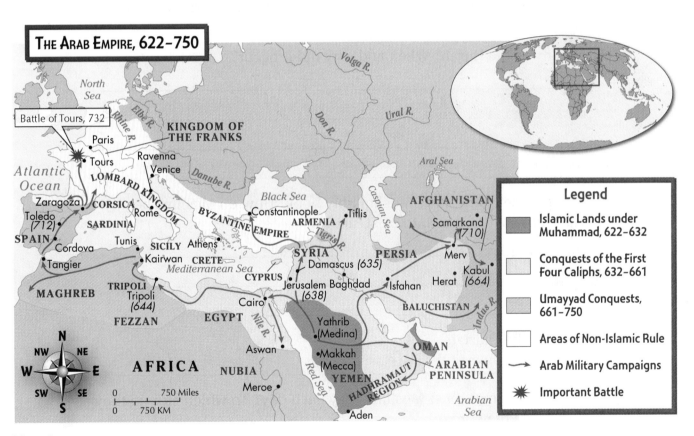

Map 2

World Religions

Something to Think About

Why is it important to respect other people's religious beliefs?

You have learned about the beginnings of Islam and how its followers built a great empire. In this activity, you will use what you learned on pages 38–41 of this lesson. Also refer to the table on the next page and the information on Appendix page 99.

1. What was the Hijrah? When and why did it occur?

_____

_____

_____

_____

2. What is the name of the Muslim holy book? How do Muslims believe their holy book came into existence?

_____

_____

_____

3. What is the Shariah?

_____

4. How many times must Muslims pray each day? To which city do they face when they pray?

_____

5. Why is the month of Ramadan important for Muslims?

_____

_____

6. One of the Five Pillars of Islam is Zakat. Describe the practice of Zakat.

_____

7. Rank the major world religions shown in the Appendix in order, from the most to the fewest number of believers.

_____

8. Use the information in the Appendix to describe one way Islam is similar to another of the major world religions. Then find one way Islam is different from another religion.

_____

_____

_____

9. Three of the major world religions described in the Appendix have their origins in the same part of the world. Name them and explain where they originated. Which is the oldest? Which is the youngest?

_____

_____

10. Use the information on Appendix page 99 and your own library research to write three paragraphs on the story of the beginnings of one of the following religions: Christianity, Hinduism, Buddhism, or Judaism. You may also choose a different religion if you wish. Write your answer on a separate piece of paper.

The Five Pillars of Islam	
Shahadah	Asserting that Allah is the only God and Muhammad is his prophet.
Salat	Performing set prayers in the direction of Mecca five times a day at specific times. Muslims must take specific postures for the prayers, which are in Arabic.
Sawm	Fasting each day during the month of Ramadan, which is the ninth month of the lunar calendar. During Ramadan, Muslims must not eat or drink between sunrise and sunset. They may eat and drink during the night, however.
Zakat	Giving 2.5 percent of one's income as alms to the poor.
Hajj	Making a pilgrimage to Mecca at least once during one's lifetime, if physically able.

Colonialism in Africa

In the late 1800s, European governments began to exert direct control over parts of Africa by establishing colonies there. This process of sending Europeans to a distant territory to gain control over its economy and politics is called **colonialism.**

King Leopold II of Belgium began the scramble to establish colonies in Africa. He was encouraged by the journeys of explorers David Livingstone and Henry Stanley in Africa's interior. Leopold II strongly believed in the importance of establishing an African empire. In 1876, he began to set up Belgian colonies in the Congo with the help of Henry Stanley. Belgium's European rivals soon began making their own claims on African territory.

A group of competing European powers came together in 1884 to develop guidelines for colonizing Africa. This **Berlin Conference** tried to regulate African trade and the areas that would be colonized. At this conference, decisions were made that led to the partition, or division, of Africa among the European powers. African leaders were not invited to the conference.

Henry Stanley explored Africa and helped establish Belgian colonies in the Congo.

Why did Europeans want to establish colonies in Africa? The reasons were mainly economic. European business owners and merchants sought new markets for their manufactured goods. Investors were looking for new places to invest their money, or capital. They were attracted by cheap labor. There was also a great demand in Europe for raw materials such as copper, cotton, tin, and rubber, which could be obtained from African colonies. Colonialism was also supported by missionaries who wanted to convert Africans to Christianity.

The development of new technology enabled the Europeans to establish their colonies. Africa is much bigger than Europe, but the development of the steamship allowed Europeans to navigate rivers far into Africa's interior. Europeans also built railroads to gain access to interior locations distant from the African coast. The development of the telegraph made communication across vast distances possible. In many cases, Europeans had to subdue a population that was hostile to them. Advancements in weaponry, such as machine guns, enabled a small, armed force of Europeans to defeat a much larger force of Africans armed only with spears. New medicines to treat tropical diseases allowed explorers to travel through unexplored areas of Africa.

European powers also had their own individual reasons for seeking control of parts of Africa. For example, Great Britain sought to control Egypt to ensure its access to the Suez Canal, an essential sea route to its colonies in India.

Most of Africa was under European control by 1902, though a few countries were able to remain independent. Ethiopia fought off an invasion by the Italians. Liberia was a colony established by Americans for former slaves and was left alone by the Europeans.

By the 1960s, most African states had achieved independence. The borders that the Europeans drew for their colonies established many of the borders used by the new independent African states. When drawing these borders, Europeans had given little thought to political alliances or rivalries among native African peoples. These artificial borders put old enemies side by side, increasing the possibility of conflict between them.

The development of the steamship allowed Europeans to navigate deep into the interior of Africa.

Build Your
Map Skills

The African Colonies

By 1914, European nations ruled nearly all of Africa. Map 1 shows the division of Africa among the European powers as of 1914. Use the map to answer the following questions.

1. On a separate piece of paper, complete a table like the one shown below, identifying all the European nations and their holdings in Africa.

European Nation	African Colonies
Great Britain	
France	
Portugal	
Spain	
Germany	
Belgium	
Italy	

2. Which European country had the largest colonies in northwest Africa?

_____

3. Which African nations were independent in 1914?

_____

4. Which European powers controlled the cities of Cairo, Tripoli, Algiers, and Mogadishu?

_____

5. In 1914, which European country controlled access to the Red Sea through the Suez Canal?

_____

6. Of the European countries with African colonies, which controlled the smallest land area of Africa?

_____

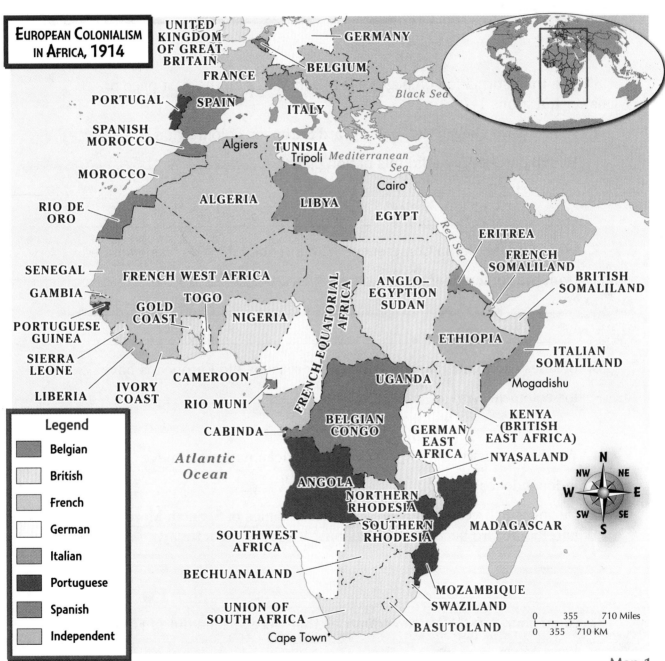

EUROPEAN COLONIALISM IN AFRICA, 1914

GERMANY
UNITED KINGDOM OF GREAT BRITAIN
FRANCE
BELGIUM
Black Sea
PORTUGAL SPAIN
ITALY
SPANISH MOROCCO
Algiers TUNISIA
Tripoli Mediterranean Sea
MOROCCO
Cairo
RIO DE ORO
ALGERIA LIBYA
EGYPT
ERITREA
FRENCH SOMALILAND
SENEGAL
FRENCH WEST AFRICA
ANGLO-EGYPTION SUDAN
BRITISH SOMALILAND
GAMBIA
TOGO
GOLD COAST
NIGERIA
PORTUGUESE GUINEA
FRENCH EQUATORIAL AFRICA
ETHIOPIA
ITALIAN SOMALILAND
SIERRA LEONE
CAMEROON
UGANDA
Mogadishu
LIBERIA IVORY COAST
RIO MUNI
CABINDA
BELGIAN CONGO
GERMAN EAST AFRICA
KENYA (BRITISH EAST AFRICA)
Atlantic Ocean
NYASALAND
ANGOLA
NORTHERN RHODESIA
SOUTHWEST AFRICA
SOUTHERN RHODESIA
MADAGASCAR
BECHUANALAND
MOZAMBIQUE
SWAZILAND
UNION OF SOUTH AFRICA
BASUTOLAND
Cape Town

Red Sea

Legend
- Belgian
- British
- French
- German
- Italian
- Portuguese
- Spanish
- Independent

N NW NE W E SW SE S

0 355 710 Miles
0 355 710 KM

Map 1

Africa Today

How has European colonialism affected nations in Africa today?

Use the information on pages 44–47 and Map 2 on the next page to answer questions 1–7.

1. Which nation began the rush toward European colonization of Africa? Which part of Africa did this nation claim? _____

   _____

   _____

2. What was the Berlin Conference? Who attended it? Who was excluded from the conference? _____

   _____

   _____

3. Besides economic reasons, what other reasons did Europeans have for colonizing Africa? _____

   _____

4. When did most west and west central African nations achieve independence? _____

5. During which years did Spain's former colonies of Spanish Morocco and Rio de Oro become independent? Describe them today.

   _____

   _____

6. Name four current African countries that were formed out of French West Africa. _____

7. What are the two newest independent African nations?

_____

Questions 8 and 9 will require library research.

8. Find out the former names of Kinshasa and Kisangani in the Democratic Republic of the Congo. Why do you think the people in the Congo changed these city names after they achieved independence?

_____

_____

_____

9. Select an African nation that has become independent since 1960. On a separate piece of paper, describe how and when the nation became independent, the country's main leaders, main economic activities, and any problems the nation has faced since becoming independent.

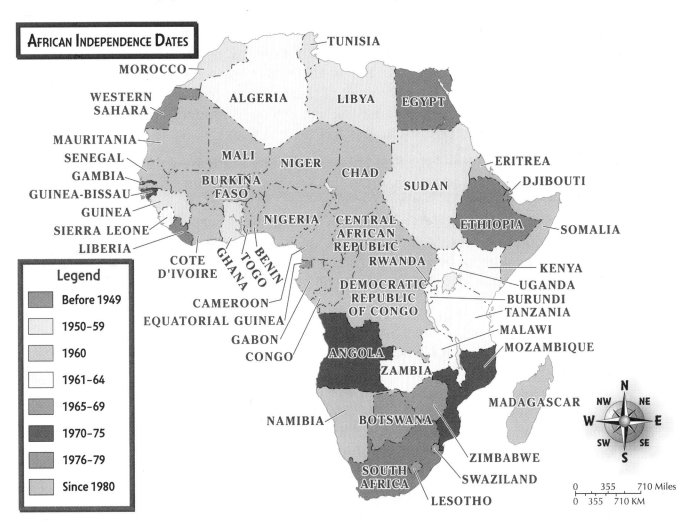

Map 2

Spain in the New World

In the 1400s, Portugal and Spain were the first European countries to claim territory in the Americas. The discoveries of Christopher Columbus for Spain created a dispute between Spain and Portugal. Both countries needed a way of dividing territory in the New World that would avoid future disputes between them.

In the **Treaty of Tordesillas** (1494), Spain and Portugal agreed on a way to settle the problem. They drew an imaginary boundary line from the North Pole to the South Pole. Lands to the east of the line would belong to Portugal; lands to the west of it would belong to Spain. This gave most of the Americas (except for Brazil) to Spain. However, because the line extended around the world, it gave more territory in Asia to Portugal.

Columbus established the first European colony in the New World on the island of Hispaniola. From this starting point, the Spanish empire spread throughout the New World to include the rest of the Caribbean Islands, Central America, and large parts of North and South America. Most of these lands were acquired for Spain by two explorers—Hernán Cortés and Francisco Pizarro. These and other Spanish explorers were called **conquistadors,** or conquerors.

In 1519, Cortés and a small Spanish force sailed from Cuba and landed on the coast of Mexico, near Veracruz. Native people called *Aztecs* had built an empire there. Cortés had the help of a group of rebellious natives. He marched to the capital city of Tenochtitlán, seized the Aztec ruler Montezuma, and demanded a ransom for him. After a terrible battle and the death of thousands, Cortés controlled the empire. The Aztecs were weakened by European diseases, including smallpox. Cortés took the Aztecs' gold and jewels and sent them to Spain. He was appointed governor of Mexico and built Mexico City where the Aztec capital had been. Most of the Aztec empire was destroyed.

Francisco Pizarro journeyed to the Incan empire in South America at a time when it was weakened by civil war. Two Incan brothers, Atahualpa and Huáscar, had fought to control the empire. Atahualpa's forces won, but thousands had been killed. At the same time, the Incas were suffering from a smallpox epidemic.

Pizarro captured Atahualpa and killed him. He then moved his army to the Incan capital, Cuzco. There, he defeated Atahualpa's forces. In 1535, Pizarro established the city of Lima. He set up a puppet Incan government. Pizarro cheated his partner of his rightful part of the Incan riches. His friend rebelled against him and was killed by Pizarro's forces in battle. In 1541, Pizarro was slain in revenge.

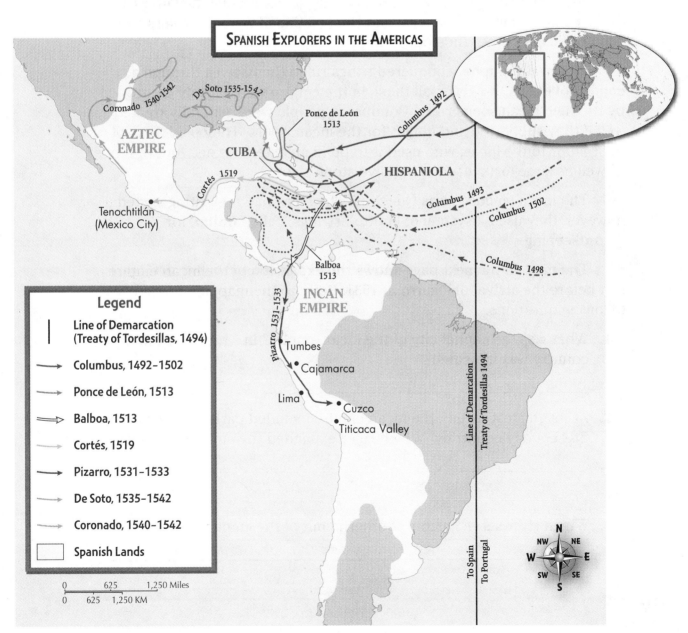

SPANISH EXPLORERS IN THE AMERICAS

Coronado 1540-1542
De Soto 1535-1542
Ponce de León 1513
Columbus 1492
AZTEC EMPIRE
CUBA
HISPANIOLA
Cortés 1519
Columbus 1493
Columbus 1502
Tenochtitlán (Mexico City)
Columbus 1498
Balboa 1513
INCAN EMPIRE
Pizarro 1531-1533
Tumbes
Cajamarca
Lima
Cuzco
Titicaca Valley
Line of Demarcation Treaty of Tordesillas 1494
To Spain
To Portugal

Legend

| Line of Demarcation (Treaty of Tordesillas, 1494)
→ Columbus, 1492–1502
→ Ponce de León, 1513
⇒ Balboa, 1513
→ Cortés, 1519
→ Pizarro, 1531–1533
→ De Soto, 1535–1542
→ Coronado, 1540–1542
☐ Spanish Lands

0   625   1,250 Miles
0   625   1,250 KM

N NE NW W E SW SE S

Build Your

The Incan Empire

Incan society began at Cuzco in the Andes Mountains of Peru in South America. From their capital city, the Incas built an empire that included millions of people and extended from modern-day Ecuador to Chile. Pachacuti Inca, Topa Inca, and Huayna Capac were the rulers who acquired most of the lands of the empire.

Within the empire, conquered tribes ruled themselves through a council of elders. However, all those in the empire were closely controlled by the rigid Incan social rules. Conquered people were generally treated well if they supported and fought for the Incan rulers. They paid a tax of their labor to the Incas, who used it to build an extensive network of roads as well as large forts made of massive stone slabs.

The Incan language was Quechua. The Incas had no writing system; however, they used a system of knotted strings, called **quipu,** for recordkeeping.

The map on the next page shows the expansion of the Incan empire just before the arrival of Pizarro in 1531. Refer to the map and answer the following questions.

1. What was the capital city of the Incan empire? In which present-day country was it located?

   _____

2. At its greatest extent, the Incan empire included parts of which present-day countries? Which ruler expanded the empire the most?

   _____

   _____

3. Which river served as the southern limit of the empire?

   _____

4. Describe how Huayna Capac extended the Incan empire.

_____

_____

_____

5. Identify three cities connected by a road built by the Incas.

_____

6. What is the highest mountain on the map? How high is it?

_____

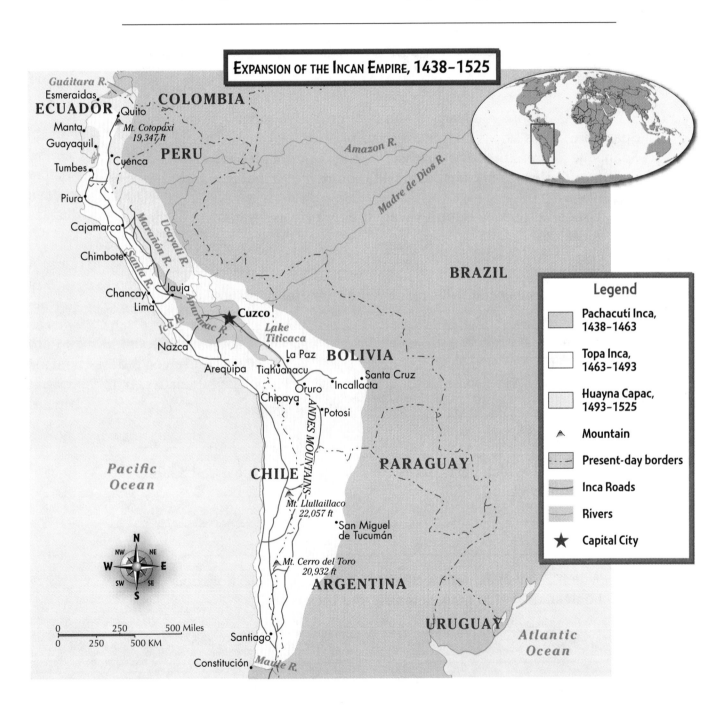

EXPANSION OF THE INCAN EMPIRE, 1438–1525

Guáitara R.
Esmeraldas
ECUADOR Quito
COLOMBIA
Manta
Guayaquil
PERU
Tumbes
Cuenca
Piura
Cajamarca
Chimbote
Chancay
Jauja
Lima
Cuzco
Nazca
Lake Titicaca
Arequipa
Tiahuanacu
Chipaya
Oruro
Incallacta
Potosi
La Paz
BOLIVIA
Santa Cruz
BRAZIL
Amazon R.
Madre de Dios R.
Marañón R.
Ucayali R.
Santa R.
Apurímac R.
Ica R.
ANDES MOUNTAINS
PARAGUAY
Pacific Ocean
CHILE
Mt. Llullaillaco 22,057 ft
San Miguel de Tucumán
Mt. Cerro del Toro 20,932 ft
ARGENTINA
URUGUAY
Atlantic Ocean
Santiago
Constitución Maule R.
Mt. Cotopáxi 19,347 ft

0   250   500 Miles
0   250   500 KM

Legend

Pachacuti Inca, 1438–1463

Topa Inca, 1463–1493

Huayna Capac, 1493–1525

▲ Mountain

Present-day borders

Inca Roads

Rivers

★ Capital City

Spanish Explorers of the Americas

How does Spanish culture influence America today?

In this lesson, you learned about some Native American empires and Spanish conquistadors. In this exercise, you will learn more about the Spanish explorers of the Americas. Use the material on pages 50–53 to answer questions 1–5. Question 6 will require additional research.

1. Which European countries were the first rivals for control of the Americas?

   _____

2. How did these countries resolve their territorial disputes?

   _____

   _____

   _____

   _____

   _____

3. In general, which parts of the New World did Portugal and Spain eventually claim?

   _____

   _____

4. Which Spanish explorers claimed the most territory for their homeland? Which native empires did they conquer?

   _____

   _____

   _____

5. Name a disease that the Spanish explorers brought with them from Europe that devastated the native peoples of the New World.

_____

6. You have learned about the explorers Cortés and Pizarro. Now select one of the other explorers shown on the map on page 51 and do some library research following these guidelines:

On a separate piece of paper, draw a detailed map of the route your explorer took to the New World and back. Include destination points, landforms and water forms encountered, cities visited (if any), and lands claimed for Spain. You can also note significant dates or events on the map. Be sure to create a map legend and compass rose.

Write a biography about your explorer in the space below. Include some facts about his early life, travels, and discoveries. Describe how the explorer treated Native Americans and how he is remembered today.

_____

_____

_____

_____

_____

_____

_____

_____

_____

_____

_____

_____

_____

_____

_____

_____

_____

LESSON 10

Building the Panama Canal

$\mathbf{A}$n **isthmus** is a narrow bridge of land linking two larger land masses. The Isthmus of Panama separates two great oceans—the Atlantic and the Pacific. In 1880, a French company began to build a canal there under the supervision of Ferdinand de Lesseps. De Lesseps had successfully directed the construction of the Suez Canal, which opened in 1869.

The French engineers who began the canal were among the finest in the world; however, they encountered great difficulties. They had underestimated the scope of the job and the difficulties of the terrain. The canal workers were afflicted with tropical diseases, including yellow fever and malaria. By the early 1890s, the effort ended in failure. Only a small part of the canal had been dug at the cost of thousands of lives and millions of dollars.

The United States considered taking over the canal project. President Theodore Roosevelt knew that there were many good reasons for the United States to build a canal to link the Atlantic and the Pacific oceans. A canal would allow ships to avoid a long and dangerous trip around Cape Horn at the southern tip of South America. Because of the increasing population in California, the United States needed an efficient transportation link to the west coast. The United States also had to consider that its navy had to defend the expanding nation in two oceans.

The Panama Canal links the Atlantic and the Pacific Oceans.

Considered one of the greatest engineering projects in history, the Panama Canal opened on August 15, 1914.

In 1902, Roosevelt bought the rights to the French canal and began negotiations with Colombia. When the negotiations stalled, the United States supported a group of Panamanian business investors who sought independence from Colombia. Panama soon became an independent nation. The new government agreed to favorable terms with the United States.

During the first year working on the canal, the Americans had the same difficulties as the French. Living conditions for the workers were terrible, and disease was rampant. A new chief engineer, John Stevens, devised a plan to improve working conditions and prevent disease. The Americans cleaned up the living areas, drained swamps, and sprayed to kill mosquitoes, which carried disease.

American engineers decided to dam the Chagres River to create Gatun Lake. They proposed the construction of a series of **locks** to enable ships to be raised to the level of Gatun Lake. The ships would then cross the lake and be lowered again to the ocean.

With this new strategy, the project made headway, but there were still great challenges. There was an elevation of the land at the Continental Divide. This area of the excavation, known as the *Culebra Cut,* required the removal of massive amounts of earth and rock. It was plagued by dangerous landslides. Eventually, all difficulties were overcome by the engineers and determination of the workers.

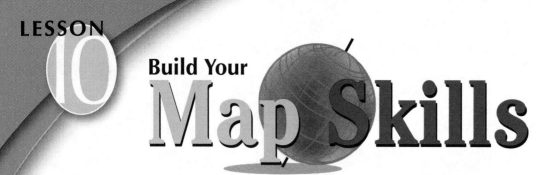

Build Your Map Skills

The Big Ditch

The Panama Canal opened on August 15, 1914. It is considered to be one of the greatest engineering projects in history. A treaty with Panama gave the United States control of a corridor of land on either side of the canal. The United States owned and operated the canal for about 85 years.

In the 1960s, Panamanians protested the presence of the United States in their country. The canal created many economic benefits for the Panamanians, but many considered the U.S. presence to be colonialism. So, in 1977, U.S. president Jimmy Carter signed a treaty with Panama to give Panama the canal by the year 2000. Today, the canal belongs to the government of Panama.

About 35 to 40 ships pass through the canal each day. The canal is almost 50 miles long, and it takes a ship 8 to 10 hours to pass through it. Locks raise the ships to the level of Gatun Lake. The ships cross the lake and are then lowered again by the locks to sea level. The locks are fed by water from Gatun Lake and Lake Alajuela (Madden Lake). Maintaining the water level in these lakes is essential to the operation of the canal.

Today, almost 100 years after its construction, the canal is still very important to the economy and national defense of the United States. It is also the pride of Panama.

Refer to the map and answer the following questions.

1. Suppose a ship is traveling from the Caribbean Sea to the Bay of Panama. In which direction would the ship be traveling? Name three locks the ship would pass through.

   _____

   _____

2. Name three defense areas (forts) in the canal area. Why do you think they are there?

   _____

   _____

3. Use the compass rose to describe the location of the capital city.

_____

_____

4. What is the name of the large island lying in the middle of Gatun Lake near the navigation channel?

_____

_____

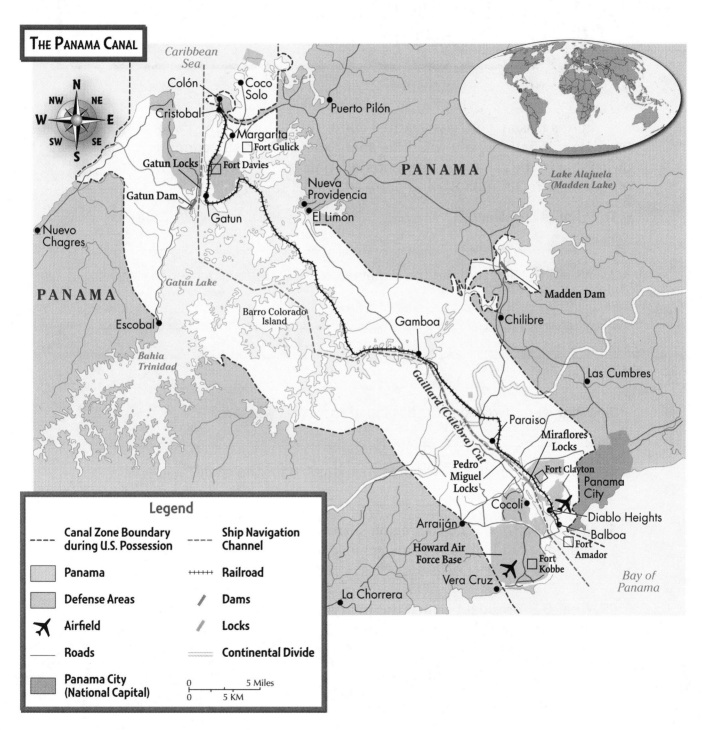

THE PANAMA CANAL

Caribbean Sea

Colón
Coco Solo
Cristobal
Puerto Pilón
Margarita
Fort Gulick
Gatun Locks
Fort Davies
PANAMA
Gatun Dam
Nueva Providencia
Gatun
El Limón
Lake Alajuela (Madden Lake)
Nuevo Chagres
Gatún Lake
PANAMA
Barro Colorado Island
Madden Dam
Escobal
Gamboa
Chilibre
Bahía Trinidad
Las Cumbres
Gaillard (Culebra) Cut
Paraiso
Miraflores Locks
Pedro Miguel Locks
Fort Clayton
Panama City
Cocoli
Diablo Heights
Arraiján
Balboa
Howard Air Force Base
Fort Amador
Fort Kobbe
Bay of Panama
Vera Cruz
La Chorrera

Legend

- - - - Canal Zone Boundary during U.S. Possession
- - - - Ship Navigation Channel

▢ Panama   +++++ Railroad

▢ Defense Areas   / Dams

✈ Airfield   / Locks

— Roads   ···· Continental Divide

▢ Panama City (National Capital)

0   5 Miles
0   5 KM

Who Should Own the Canal?

How have the actions of the United States affected Latin America?

In this lesson, you have learned about the history of the Panama Canal. In this activity, you will think about some issues surrounding ownership of the canal. Use the material on pages 56–59 to answer questions 1–7. Question 8 will require additional research.

1. What is an isthmus?

   _____

2. Who first tried to build the Panama Canal? Did they succeed? Why or why not?

   _____

   _____

   _____

3. What were two diseases that killed the canal workers?

   _____

4. Which U.S. president was most responsible for the canal?

   _____

5. What country owned the region surrounding the canal before the United States helped Panama achieve independence?

   _____

6. What U.S. president signed the treaty to give the canal back to Panama? In which year did Panama get ownership of the canal zone?

   _____

7. What was happening in Africa at about the time the Panama Canal was being built? (Reread Lesson 8 on pages 44–49 to refresh your memory.) Do you see any similarities between what European countries were doing in Africa and what the United States was doing in Panama? Explain.

_____

_____

_____

_____

8. You will now take on the role of an assistant to a U.S. senator in the 1970s. You have been assigned to research the arguments for and against returning the canal to Panama. Use the library to learn as much as you can about the issue. Then, write at least one paragraph in favor of the idea and one paragraph against it. Be sure to cite your reasons.

As you conduct your research and form your arguments, think of the following questions:

- Which cultures and governments were affected the most by the building of the canal? How?

- Did the United States gain the land surrounding the canal in a fair and ethical way? Why or why not?

- Who worked on the canal? What dangers did they face?

- How did the Panama Canal Treaty of 1903 affect U.S.-Panama relations? How did it affect U.S. relations with other Central American nations?

- What effect did the building of the Canal have on a U.S. presence in Central America?

- Who prospered as a result of the Panama Canal?

_____

_____

_____

_____

_____

_____

_____

LESSON 11

The Struggle for Europe

In the spring of 1944, most of Europe remained under the strict control of Adolf Hitler, the leader of Nazi Germany. The Allied powers, including the United States, Britain, Canada, and other countries, developed a plan to invade France and liberate western Europe. The invasion was called **Operation Overlord.** The first day of the operation was referred to as **D-Day.**

The invasion of France would be by sea, across the English Channel. It would be the largest invasion of its type in history, involving about 3 million men and women, 5,000 ships, and 11,000 aircraft.

The supreme commander of the invasion forces was U.S. general Dwight D. Eisenhower. Eisenhower and other planners knew that they had to keep German forces guessing about where the invasion would take place. The real location had to be kept secret, otherwise, the Germans could concentrate their troops where the Allied forces would land and possibly drive them away.

To prepare for the invasion, Allied forces were massed at bases all along the southern coast of Britain. Considering this, the most logical place for the invasion to take place was at Pas de Calais on the French coast. Pas de Calais was the shortest point across the English Channel, and it had excellent beaches for the large operation. The Germans knew this, and they had strong defenses at that location.

General Dwight D. Eisenhower became the thirty-fourth president of the United States, 1953–1961.

Through false messages, the Allies tricked the Germans into thinking they intended to land at Pas de Calais and also in Norway. The real invasion would be far to the south in France at Normandy on the Cotentin Peninsula.

This strategy of deception was also intended to confuse the Germans so they would delay their response to the invasion. This trick would allow the Allies to get a foothold on the beaches from which they could launch their operations inland.

The D-Day invasion was a huge and difficult undertaking, but it was successful. However, the Allies still faced the battle for Normandy. At first, the Allies advanced very slowly against the German defenses. They were delayed by hedgerows of brush between fields that worked as good German defensive positions.

General Omar Bradley devised a plan code-named *Operation Cobra* to force a breakout from the Cotentin Peninsula. Supported by a massive Allied bombing effort, the operation was much more successful than expected. The German defenses collapsed. Soon, the Allies poured across northern France. By the end of August, the Allies had liberated Paris.

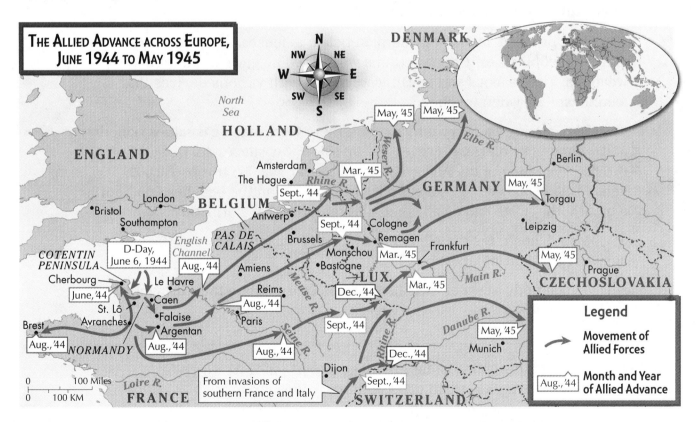

Map 1

Build Your

The Invasion at Normandy

The Allied invasion of France took place on June 6, 1944. There were five separate beachheads, or landing areas. They were code-named *Utah, Omaha, Gold, Juno,* and *Sword.* Before the landing, airborne troops, called *paratroopers,* parachuted from airplanes behind enemy lines to secure bridges and other important sites to prepare for the invasion. Also, gliders containing additional troops landed behind enemy lines.

The invasion planners knew they needed a full moon for the invasion to be a success because this would produce a favorable **ocean tide,** or sea depth, at the landing location. The full moon would also provide light for the troops in the early morning hours.

Troops faced a variety of German beach defenses. They included concrete pillboxes for German troops with machine guns and antitank weapons. The beaches and ocean were mined with various devices that would explode when touched.

The landing was very difficult, and there were many casualties (killed and wounded soldiers). However, the invasion was successful because of the determination of the Allies. By June 11, over 300,000 troops, 50,000 vehicles, and 100,000 tons of supplies had landed on the beaches. In about a month, the Allies had established a firm foothold in Normandy.

Map 2 illustrates the Allied invasion at Normandy. Refer to the map to answer the following questions.

1. Which body of water did Allied troops cross during the Normandy invasion?

   _____

2. At which beachheads did American troops land? At which beachheads did British and Canadian troops land?

   _____

   _____

3. Which American and British Airborne divisions made landings at Normandy? Near which beachheads did each land?

_____

_____

4. Which French towns were heavily fortified by the Germans with mine fields?

_____

_____

5. In which direction is Paris, France, from the beaches at Normandy?

_____

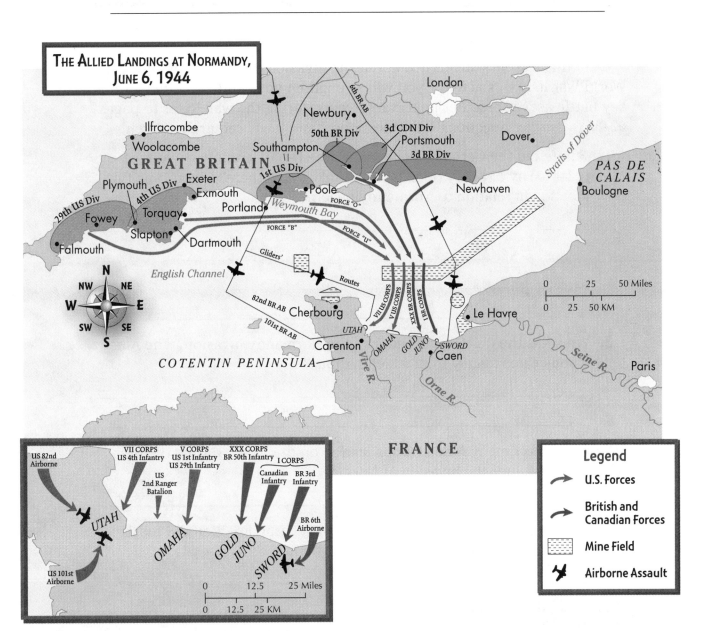

Map 2

World War II: The European Theatre

Something to Think About

Why is it important to understand the events that occur during war?

In this lesson, you learned about the invasion at Normandy during World War II. In this activity, you will strengthen your understanding of this key battle as well as other important events during the war. Refer to pages 62–65 to answer questions 1–6. Questions 7 and 8 will require research.

1. Where did the Germans believe that the D-Day landing would take place? Why did they think it would take place there? Where was this location in relation to Normandy beach?

   _____

   _____

   _____

   _____

2. Who was the chief commander of the Normandy invasion? The Allied troops came mainly from which nations?

   _____

   _____

3. About how many Allied troops landed on the beach during the first five days after the invasion at Normandy?

   _____

4. After the Normandy invasion, in which general direction did most Allied troops turn and advance through France?

   _____

5. When did Allied troops cross the Rhine River at Remagen?

   _____

6. When did Allied invasion forces from southern France and Italy cross into Germany?

_____

7. Use the timeline on page 100 of the Appendix to place the following events in chronological order. Write a "1" in the space beside the first event; write a "2" beside the second event, and so on.

_____ Winston Churchill becomes new Prime Minister of Britain.

_____ Paris is liberated.

_____ Allies land on Italian mainland.

_____ Munich Agreement sacrifices Czechoslovakia to Hitler.

_____ German troops annex Austria.

_____ Germany invades Soviet Union.

_____ Germany invades and conquers Poland.

_____ Adolf Hitler becomes new Chancellor of Germany.

_____ Allies invade Sicily.

_____ France surrenders to Germany.

_____ Germany and Italy declare war on United States.

_____ Allies defeat Germans at the Battle of the Bulge.

_____ Battle of Stalingrad.

_____ Ethiopia surrenders to Italian forces.

_____ Battle of Britain (German air raids on British Isles).

_____ Mussolini comes to power in Italy.

_____ Germany surrenders to the Allies.

_____ British defeat Germans at El Alamein.

_____ Italy and Germany form Rome-Berlin Axis.

_____ Allies invade Normandy.

8. Select one of the events from question 7 and do some library research to learn more about it. Write at least three paragraphs about the event on a separate piece of paper. Explain what happened, why it happened, and why it was important.

The Cold War

After the close of World War II, war-ravaged Europe fell under the influence of the occupying powers. The United States and Great Britain wanted to establish democratic governments in many of the Eastern European countries that were occupied by the Union of Soviet Socialist Republics (Soviet Union). Political conflicts arose that resulted in mutual fear, distrust, and rivalry between the Soviets and the West. These conflicts led to a long-term division of Europe and political tensions that became known as the **Cold War.**

In 1949, to protect their interests, the United States and some Western European nations formed the **North Atlantic Treaty Organization (NATO)** for mutual defense. In response, the Soviet Union formed the **Warsaw Pact** in 1955. Both the United States and the Soviet Union engaged in an arms race that resulted in the manufacture of great numbers of nuclear weapons. Because both sides feared the possible results of a direct war, the United States and the the Soviets participated in proxy wars in which third parties did the actual fighting.

During the Cold War, most of Eastern Europe and the Balkans (except for Albania, Yugoslavia, and Greece) fell under strict Soviet control. The Soviets established a one-party communist system in these satellite states. Due to their political and economic isolation, these Eastern European states became known as countries of the **Iron Curtain.** The Soviet Union put down dissident movements with military force when they challenged communist authority. This Soviet policy was known as the **Brezhnev Doctrine** (named after Leonid Brezhnev, who ruled the Soviet Union from 1964 to 1982).

June 26, 1963 President John F. Kennedy inspects the Berlin Wall during a visit to West Berlin.

During the Cold War, the East German Communists erected a wall separating East Germany from West Germany. It stopped emigration and split many families.

The Soviet style of government was one of strong, central control. Rather than depending upon market forces, a huge bureaucracy dictated the types of goods that would be manufactured and consumed. This discouraged hard work and efficiency. By the 1970s, the Communist rulers had become a corrupt, elite class that enjoyed a high standard of living in a declining nation. Hoping to change this situation, a group of reformers in the Soviet Communist Party chose Mikhail Gorbachev as leader in 1985.

Gorbachev called his program of reforms **perestroika,** or restructuring. He wanted to change the Soviet economic system to a market economy permitting private business ownership. This led to political reform that allowed political parties other than the Communist Party to have power. This relaxation of authority began to encourage nationalist movements throughout the Soviet Union. By 1990, Estonia, Latvia, Georgia, Lithuania, and many other Soviet states had developed strong independence movements. Throughout the Soviet Union, independence movements were also encouraged by the many different nationalities, cultures, and ethnic backgrounds that were under Soviet authority.

In 1991, a group of Soviet leaders arrested Gorbachev and tried to reestablish the old authoritarian regime. However, thousands of Russians rallied to resist. After Ukraine and other Soviet states voted for independence, the Soviet Union was dissolved.

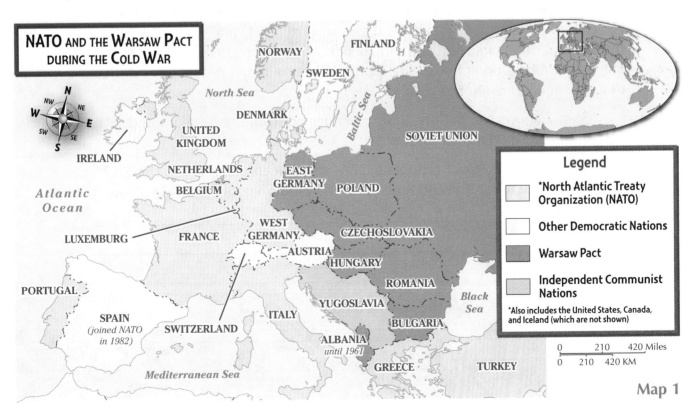

Map 1

Build Your

Map Skills

The Commonwealth of Independent States

After the collapse of the Soviet Union, an alliance of former Soviet republics, named the *Commonwealth of Independent States* (CIS), was founded on December 8, 1991. Members included Belarus, Ukraine, Russia, Armenia, Azerbaijan, Kazakhstan, Kyrgyzstan, Moldova, Tajikistan, Turkmenistan, and Uzbekistan. Georgia joined in 1993. (The former Soviet republics of Estonia, Latvia, and Lithuania declined to join the commonwealth.) The headquarters of the CIS is in Minsk, Belarus.

Members of the CIS operate as independent nations. The CIS is an economic union intended to help encourage and regulate trade. It also attempts to deal with security issues, finance, and law. Though members are independent, the CIS has been criticized by some as simply a way for Russia to maintain some measure of control over former regions of the Soviet Union.

The future of the CIS has been questioned by some member states. For example, Georgia has made gestures toward NATO and withdrew from the Council of Defense Ministers in 2006. Ukraine is considering halting its financial contributions to CIS. In addition, Turkmenistan reduced its status to an associate member in 2005.

Map 2 shows the nations that were formed from the breakup of the Soviet Union. Use the map to answer the following questions.

1. Which former Soviet republics have never been members of the CIS? Name one thing these nations have in common geographically.

_____

_____

_____

2. After Russia, what is the largest nation in the CIS?

_____

3. Which CIS members probably profit the most from trade through the Black Sea? How do you know?

_____

_____

4. Which four CIS members share a border with China?

_____

5. Which three CIS members lie closest to Europe?

_____

6. Which CIS nations are landlocked (that is, have no access to an ocean)? (Note that the Aral and Caspian seas do not provide ocean access.)

_____

_____

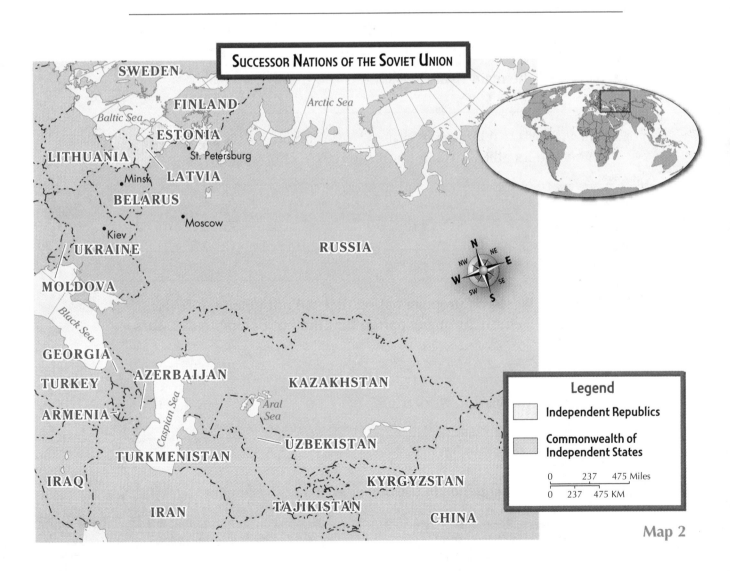

SUCCESSOR NATIONS OF THE SOVIET UNION

SWEDEN
FINLAND
Arctic Sea
Baltic Sea
ESTONIA
LITHUANIA
St. Petersburg
LATVIA
Minsk
BELARUS
Moscow
Kiev
UKRAINE
RUSSIA
MOLDOVA
Black Sea
GEORGIA
TURKEY
AZERBAIJAN
KAZAKHSTAN
Caspian Sea
Aral Sea
ARMENIA
UZBEKISTAN
TURKMENISTAN
IRAQ
KYRGYZSTAN
IRAN
TAJIKISTAN
CHINA

N NE E SE S SW W NW

Legend

Independent Republics

Commonwealth of Independent States

0   237   475 Miles
0   237   475 KM

Map 2

Struggles in the Soviet Satellite States

Something to **Think** About

How have the struggles of the Soviet satellite states affected American history?

In this activity, you will learn more about freedom movements in Eastern Europe and the current status of the former Soviet republics. Use the material on pages 68–71 and Appendix page 101 to answer questions 1–7. Questions 8–9 will require additional research.

1. Who were the main rivals in the Cold War?

_____

2. What is NATO? Why was it formed? What organization did the Soviet Union and its allies form in response to NATO?

_____

_____

_____

_____

3. Name one Western European nation that did not belong to NATO. Name one Eastern European nation that did not belong to the Warsaw Pact.

_____

4. What was the Brezhnev Doctrine?

_____

_____

5. Name one consequence of the Soviet style of government.

_____

_____

6. What was perestroika? Perestroika began under whose leadership? What did it bring about?

_____

_____

_____

_____

7. Which was the first Soviet republic to declare its independence? Besides Russia itself, which was the last?

_____

Do some library research to answer the following questions.

8. Before the breakup of the Soviet Union, the Soviets put down challenges to Communist authority in their satellite states. Select one of the following dissident movements and write three paragraphs about it on a separate piece of paper. In your paper, discuss what happened, when and where it happened, why it happened, who the principal leaders were, and how it turned out.

| East German Uprising of 1953 | Prague Spring (1968) |
| Hungarian Revolution (1956) | Polish Solidarity movement (1980s) |

9. Select one of the countries that formed after the breakup of the Soviet Union (see the list on Appendix page 101). Find the following information for that country. If necessary, record your answers on a separate piece of paper. (For "Ethnic tensions or international disputes," note any ethnic tension within the country or problems the country is having with other nations.)

- **Country:**
- **Date of independence:**
- **Natural resources:**
- **Main imports and exports:**
- **Primary ethnic groups:**
- **Ethnic tensions or international disputes:**

Ecoregions of the World

Scientists that study Earth sometimes organize the planet into zones according to the types of **organisms** (plants and animals) that live in each area and the kind of weather that occurs there. One common division that scientists use is the ecoregion, or ecological region. An **ecoregion** is a geographical area with similar ecosystems. An ecosystem is an area of land or water that has a collection of plants and animals that is unique to that area. These plants and animals are dependent upon one another for their survival.

Terrestrial ecoregions are those that are on land. A desert is an example of a terrestrial ecoregion. Aquatic ecoregions are those that are in water. Lakes and wetlands are examples of aquatic ecoregions.

The types of plants that can live in an ecoregion are determined by climate. **Climate** is the usual pattern of weather in a particular place, including precipitation. **Elevation** (height in relation to sea level) and soil type also affect the types of plants that can grow in an ecoregion because elevation affects temperature. Ecoregions are roughly related to the lines of latitude, and this also indicates that they are linked to climate.

Both plants and animals adapt to their environment. For example, cactuses have adapted to the dry environment of the desert by storing water in their succulent stems and leaves. The types of plants in an ecoregion determine what kind of animals can live there.

Cactuses have adapted to their environment by storing water in their succulent stems and leaves.

Ecoregions help scientists and government leaders develop conservation plans that help to maintain biodiversity in an area. The term **biodiversity,** or biological diversity, refers to the variety of plant and animal species living in a certain area. A conservation plan helps to preserve **habitat,** or the places where plants and animals live. A conservation plan helps to identify animals and plants that may become endangered and helps to ensure that these organisms are not destroyed.

There are many different ways that an ecosystem may become endangered. Some ecoregions are threatened by **invasive** (non-native) **species.** These are types of plants or animals that have been introduced to an area where they do not occur naturally. They may eventually displace or destroy the native plants or animals of an ecoregion. Most invasive species are intentionally or unintentionally introduced to an area by human beings. For example, the brown tree snake on the Pacific island of Guam has almost completely destroyed most native bird species on that island. It was probably unintentionally transported there on a cargo ship.

Ecosystems can become endangered through overuse by human beings. For example, the populations of many types of fish that are used for food, such as tuna and cod, have been endangered from overfishing. Some scientists think that fishing boats dragging the bottom of the ocean with nets might be destroying biodiversity in some aquatic ecosystems.

The boreal forest is one of the world's largest terrestrial ecoregions.

Due to overfishing, the populations of certain types of fish have been declining.

Build Your

Ecoregions on a World Map

Different plants grow in different ecoregions. For example, deciduous trees typically grow in temperate, mid-latitude ecoregions that do not experience wide temperature changes. **Deciduous trees** produce leaves, which they usually drop every fall. Northern ecoregions support more **coniferous trees,** which produce needles rather than leaves. Map 1 illustrates and describes the different ecoregions of the world. Use the map to answer the questions. Also refer to Appendix page 102.

1. Which areas of the world have tropical rainforests?

_____

_____

_____

2. Which ecoregion predominates in Europe? Where can this ecoregion be found in North America?

_____

_____

3. Which two continents have the most desert in proportion to their total land area?

_____

4. Which ecoregions occupy most of the lands north of 60° N latitude?

_____

5. Describe one difference between most trees growing in the eastern part of the United States and those that grow in Canada.

_____

_____

_____

6. Mediterranean ecoregions are generally found between which degrees of latitude?

_____

7. Which area gets the most rain: a tropical deciduous forest, a boreal forest, or a tropical rainforest? Which gets the least?

_____

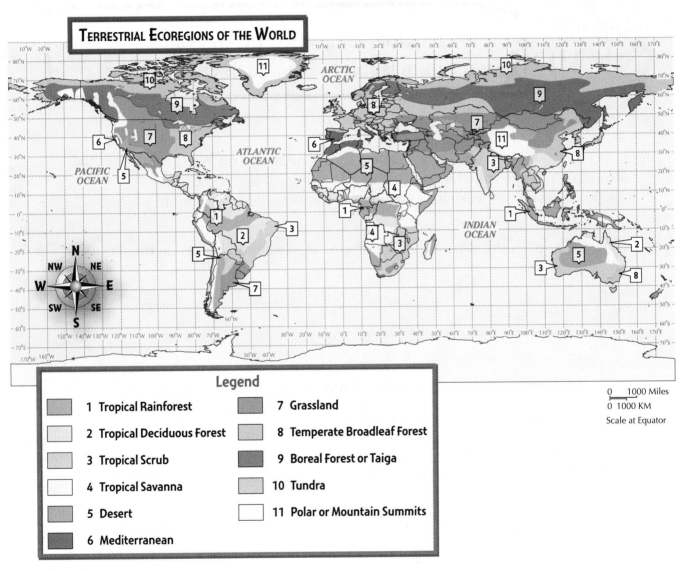

Map 1

How Organisms Adapt

What factors could affect the ways an organism is able to adapt to its environment?

In this lesson, you have learned about the world's ecoregions. After strengthening your understanding of this material, you will do some library research to learn how different organisms have adapted to each ecoregion.

1. What does the word *ecoregion* mean? How would you define the word *ecoregion?*

_____

_____

_____

2. What determines the types of plants that can live in an ecoregion?

_____

_____

3. What is biodiversity? Identify an ecoregion with rich biodiversity and one with less rich biodiversity.

_____

_____

_____

_____

4. What are invasive species and how can they hurt ecoregions?

_____

_____

_____

5. Name one way rainfall in a tropical deciduous forest differs from rainfall in a temperate broadleaf forest.

_____

_____

_____

6. Name a difference between tropical savanna and grassland ecoregions.

_____

7. Name one ecoregion that does not support trees of any kind.

_____

8. Now do some library research to complete the following table. Find a plant or animal that lives in each ecoregion. Describe one way the organism has adapted to its environment.

Ecoregion	Organism	Adaptation to Environment
Tropical Rainforest		
Tropical Deciduous Forest		
Tropical Scrub		
Tropical Savanna		
Desert		
Mediterranean		
Grassland		
Temperate Broadleaf Forest		
Boreal Forest/Taiga		
Tundra		
Polar or Mountain Summits		

The Need for Energy

We all use energy. Every time you listen to a CD, play a video game, or take a car ride, you are using energy. When you turn on a light or turn up the air conditioning, you are using energy. People in the United States and other industrialized nations expect that energy will be readily available whenever they want it. Think about how you felt the last time the electricity went out during a thunderstorm.

Did you ever wonder where all that energy comes from? There are two broad categories of energy: renewable and nonrenewable. **Renewable energy** sources can keep producing indefinitely without being used up. Examples include solar power, wind power, and hydropower. **Nonrenewable energy** sources, by contrast, will eventually be used up. Examples include fossil fuels such as oil (petroleum), natural gas, and coal.

Fossil fuels were formed from the remains of prehistoric plants and animals. They use combustion—the process of burning—to create energy. Power plants burn fossil fuels to supply heat and electricity for homes and businesses. Gasoline and diesel fuel, made from crude oil, are used to power cars, buses, and trucks. Heating oil and electricity from power plants are used to heat homes and businesses.

Large tankers are used to transport oil around the world.

Currently, most of the world's energy is provided by nonrenewable sources. The world economy runs on oil, coal, and natural gas. For example, 97 percent of the energy used for transportation in the United States (that is, cars, buses, subways, railroads, airplanes, and so on) comes from fuels made from oil. In all, fossil fuels supply about 85 percent of the total amount of energy we use in the United States.

Coal is a fossil fuel widely used to supply energy.

The use of nonrenewable energy sources creates a variety of problems. For one thing, the combustion of fossil fuels creates air pollution. Also, much of the oil used in the world economy comes from just a handful of countries. Some of these countries are in politically unstable areas of the world. Changes in these countries could potentially reduce the world's supply of oil, hurting the world economy.

Despite all this, the demand for fossil fuels is growing. The table summarizes the expected fuel mix for the generation of electricity worldwide by the year 2025 (measured in gigawatts). Much of the increased demand is occurring in developing nations. In China, for example, the number of cars has been growing by 20 percent every year. New airports are being built in these countries, expanding jet fuel demand. More manufacturing jobs in developing nations will mean larger amounts of energy for factories and transportation. Fossil fuels will remain the chief energy source for the world's economy for the foreseeable future.

Fuel Type	2002	Projected Electricity Consumption Worldwide (in gigawatts*)			
		2010	2015	2020	2025
Natural gas and oil	1,207	1,851	2,071	2,304	2,580
Coal	987	1,151	1,232	1,322	1,403
Nuclear	361	390	401	411	422
Renewable	763	927	980	1,036	1,110
Total	3,318	4,319	4,684	5,073	5,495

*A watt is a measure of the power produced as electricity. For example, a household light bulb uses about 100 watts of electricity. A gigawatt is equal to 1 billion watts.

Source: The U.S. Department of Energy

Build Your
Map Skills

A World Oil Map and Chart

The estimated amount of oil a country could take from the ground in the future is called its **oil reserves. Oil consumption** refers to the amount of oil used. Like most countries in the industrialized world, the United States uses much more oil than it can produce on its own. For this reason, the United States must buy much of its oil from foreign countries. This creates a certain amount of political and economic risk.

For example, the United States must stay on friendly terms with the countries that supply it with oil; otherwise, those countries could slow down or stop the flow of oil. Because so much of the American economy runs on oil, the countries that supply the United States with this resource have a major influence on the national economy. If oil-producing countries raise their prices for oil, prices for things you buy every day could go up.

The map and chart show the amount of oil reserves in the world and the amount of daily consumption. Use them to answer the following questions.

1. Which region of the world holds the most oil reserves? What percentage of the world's oil is in this region?

   _____

   _____

2. Which region of the world uses most of the world's oil? What percentage of the world's oil does this region use?

   _____

   _____

3. Which region of the world has the least oil reserves? How do you think this affects the region's economy?

   _____

   _____

   _____

4. Besides the Middle East, which regions of the world probably ship oil to other nations? Why do you think this may be so?

_____

_____

_____

_____

5. Which region has the world's second-largest oil consumption?

_____

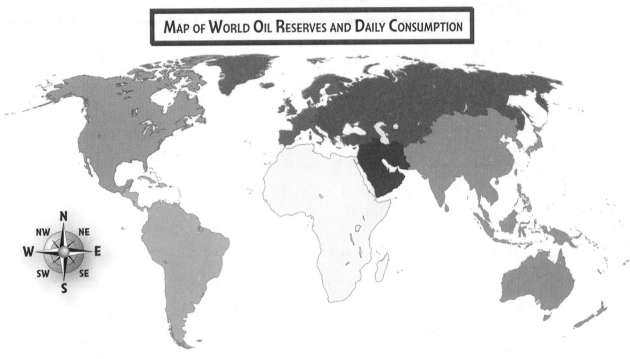

MAP OF WORLD OIL RESERVES AND DAILY CONSUMPTION

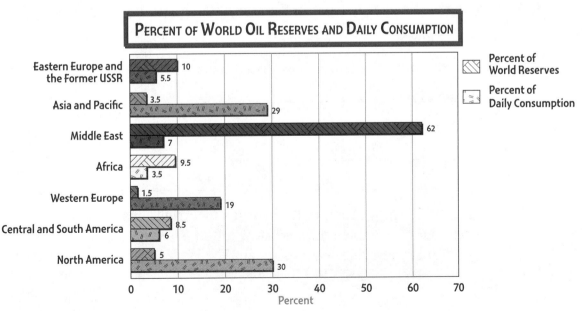

PERCENT OF WORLD OIL RESERVES AND DAILY CONSUMPTION

Percent of World Reserves

Percent of Daily Consumption

Region	Percent of World Reserves	Percent of Daily Consumption
Eastern Europe and the Former USSR	10	5.5
Asia and Pacific	3.5	29
Middle East	62	7
Africa	9.5	3.5
Western Europe	1.5	19
Central and South America	8.5	6
North America	5	30

Percent

Energy Issues

 Something to Think About

How do you think the world's energy needs will be met 100 years from now?

Review the information on pages 80–83 and answer the following questions.

1. What is a difference between renewable and nonrenewable energy sources? _____

_____

_____

2. What are fossil fuels? How are they used to create energy? _____

_____

_____

_____

3. How much of the energy used in the United States today is generated from fossil fuels? _____

4. Name two reasons why demand for fossil fuels is expected to increase over the next few decades. _____

_____

_____

5. As of 2002, about how much of the world's electricity was being produced from renewable sources? How much is expected to be produced from renewable sources by 2025?

_____

_____

Perform your own library research to answer the questions below.

6. At current rates of consumption, how long is the world's reserve of oil expected to last? How long will reserves of natural gas last?

_____

_____

_____

7. Think about what you have learned about fossil fuels in this lesson. Then, describe one scientific and one political reason why the United States should consider developing renewable energy technologies.

_____

_____

8. Complete the table below about some of the renewable sources of energy. Briefly describe how each type of energy works and list some advantages and disadvantages of each. After you have filled in the information below, write one paragraph, on a separate piece of paper, describing which source of renewable energy has the best chance of being used widely throughout the United States and why.

Renewable Energy Source	How Does It Work?	Advantages	Disadvantages
Wind Power			
Hydropower			
Solar Power			

Sea Ice of the Arctic

The Arctic region is about 1.5 times the size of the United States. At the center of this vast region is the Arctic Ocean, which is an ocean of ice surrounded by islands and continental land masses. The Greenland Sea and the Davis Strait connect the Arctic Ocean to the Atlantic Ocean, and the Bering Strait connects it to the Pacific Ocean. The Arctic Ocean is the smallest of the world's oceans, though it covers over 5 million square miles.

Due to the tilt of Earth on its axis as it orbits the sun, the Arctic experiences extended periods of darkness in winter; likewise, it experiences long periods of continuous light in the summer.

The Arctic can be considered to be the area north of the Arctic Circle, which is 66.5 degrees north latitude. However, some scientists think the Arctic is better described as the area north of the tree line, or the point where the treeless tundra begins. The tundra just south of the Arctic region is mostly plains where trees cannot grow due to high winds and cold temperatures. This is also the point where the 50-degree Fahrenheit isotherm begins—north of this point summer temperatures average no higher than 50 degrees.

The Arctic is covered with ice about nine months per year. About half of that ice melts in the summer months. Some ice in the Arctic Sea melts and refreezes every year. Other ice, called **perennial sea ice,** remains frozen all year. In summer, the ice pack is surrounded by open seas; however, in the winter, the sea is mostly locked in ice all the way to the landmasses of the surrounding continents. The ice averages about 10 feet in thickness but can be up to 30 feet thick.

Scientists have detected what they believe is a trend in the melting of the perennial sea ice during the summer months. About 9 percent more of the ice pack is melting every decade when compared with the previous decade. Why are scientists concerned about this? Some see it as evidence of global climate change. Scientists are concerned because the Arctic ice reflects the sun's rays and helps keep the sun from warming Earth. Areas of open water not covered by ice tend to absorb the sun's heat. Thus, the warming of Earth could accelerate as the Arctic ice is lost. If enough Arctic ice is lost, this could affect the plants and animals that live there.

At the most basic level, life in the Arctic depends on the plankton and algae that develop on the ice and in the water there. A big change in the amount of sea ice could change how these important organisms grow. The animals that need the ice for survival could be affected, too. For example, polar bears and seals use the ice to reach the sea where they feed. A reduced population of seals and other mammals could also hurt native people who hunt them for food.

What is causing the warming of the Arctic? Some scientists think that it is caused by long-term climate cycles that bring warm air and water into the region. Others believe that it is partly caused by greenhouse gases that humans release into the atmosphere by burning fossil fuels such as coal and oil.

Seals and polar bears live on the Arctic Sea ice.

Build Your

Map of the Arctic

The Arctic is generally the region surrounding Earth's North Pole, or the northernmost point on the planet. The Arctic Circle forms the boundary within which the north experiences the midnight sun (24 hours of sun about June 21) and the polar night (24 hours of darkness about December 22). Use the map to answer the following questions.

1. Identify all the seas within the Arctic Circle that border Russia.

_____

_____

2. Which body of water separates Baffin Island from Greenland?

_____

3. Use the map to identify three outlets from the Arctic Ocean to either the Atlantic or the Pacific Ocean.

_____

4. Name three major rivers that flow into the Arctic Ocean and the countries through which they flow.

_____

_____

5. Name the countries that have lands on or within the Arctic Circle.

_____

_____

_____

6. Name four cities that lie within the Arctic Circle.

_____

_____

_____

7. The Arctic Circle is the traditional boundary for the Arctic region. Identify one body of water, one city, and one island that are not within the Arctic Circle but which would be considered "Arctic" if the 50 degree Fahrenheit isotherm were used as the boundary line.

_____

_____

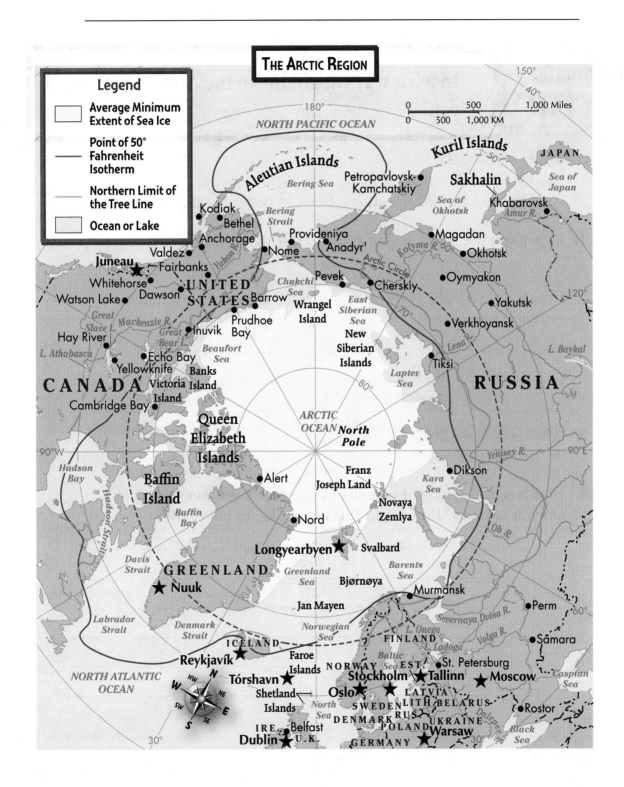

THE ARCTIC REGION

Legend

Average Minimum Extent of Sea Ice

Point of 50° Fahrenheit Isotherm

Northern Limit of the Tree Line

Ocean or Lake

Life in the Arctic

Something to **Think** About

In what ways might life in the Arctic affect you?

Answer the following questions. Refer to pages 86–89, if necessary.

1. How big is the Arctic region compared with the United States?

    _____

2. How long each year is the Arctic covered with ice? How much melts during the summer?

    _____

    _____

    _____

3. What is the tree line?

    _____

4. How has the melting of perennial sea ice changed over the past several decades? How might this impact life in the Arctic?

    _____

    _____

    _____

    _____

    _____

    _____

5. The table briefly describes the three biological communities, or realms, of the Arctic Ocean. The diagram illustrates a **food web** involving some of the organisms of the various realms. The arrows in the diagram indicate that the polar bear feeds on the seal, which feeds on the arctic cod, which feeds on under-ice crustaceans and gelatinous zooplankton.

Do library research to create your own Arctic food-web diagram on a separate sheet of paper. You should use at least one organism from each realm; use more if you like. Label each realm and each organism.

Name	Description	Examples
Sea-Ice Realm	Includes organisms that live in, on, and just under arctic ice	Diatoms, algae, bacteria, viruses, fungi, polar bears, arctic cod
Pelagic Realm	Includes organisms that live between the ocean surface and the ocean bottom	Zooplankton, fish, squids, seals, whales
Benthic Realm	Includes organisms that live on the ocean bottom	Sponges, bivalves, crustaceans, sea anemones

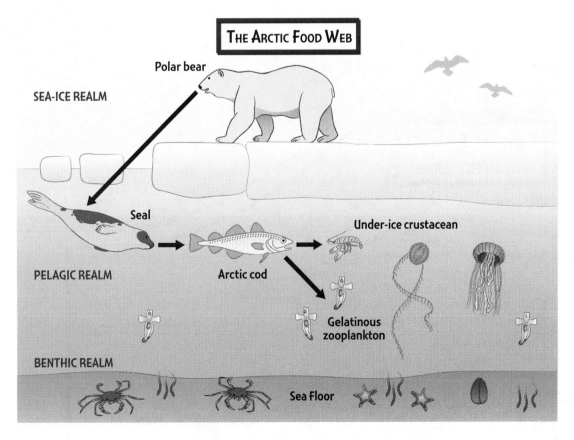

THE ARCTIC FOOD WEB

Polar bear

SEA-ICE REALM

Seal

PELAGIC REALM

Arctic cod

Under-ice crustacean

Gelatinous zooplankton

BENTHIC REALM

Sea Floor

Appendix

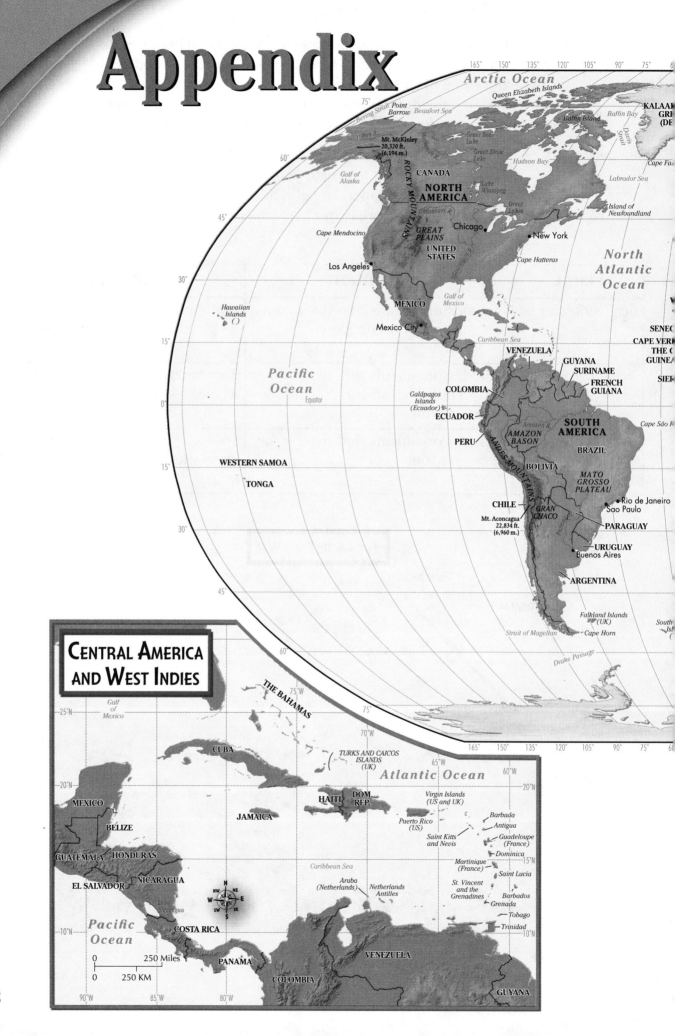

CENTRAL AMERICA AND WEST INDIES

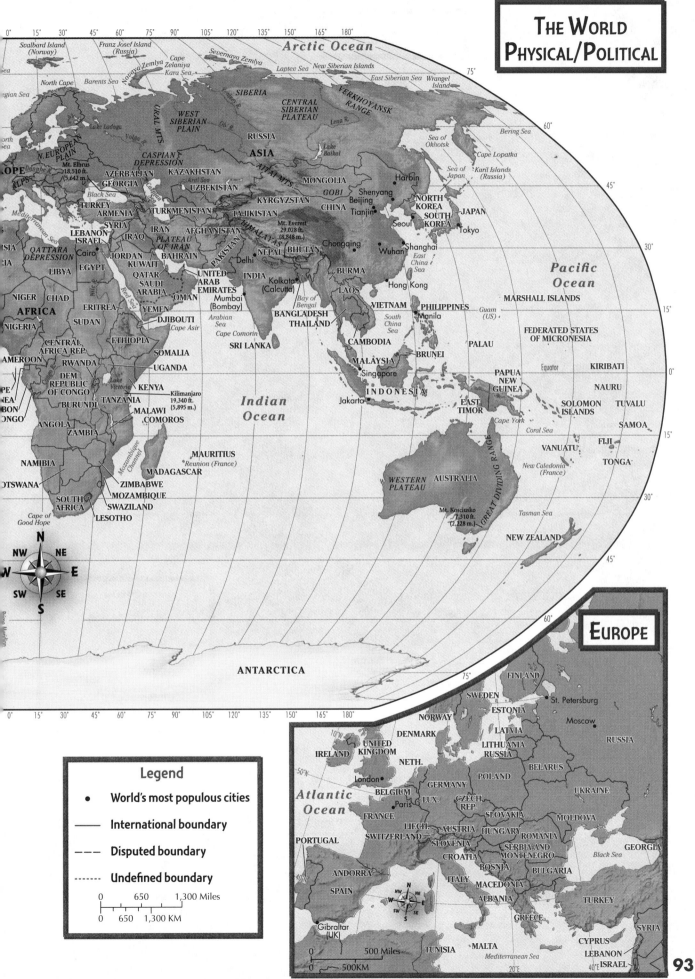

EUROPE

Legend

- • World's most populous cities
- — International boundary
- – – – Disputed boundary
- ...... Undefined boundary

0   650   1,300 Miles

0   650   1,300 KM

93

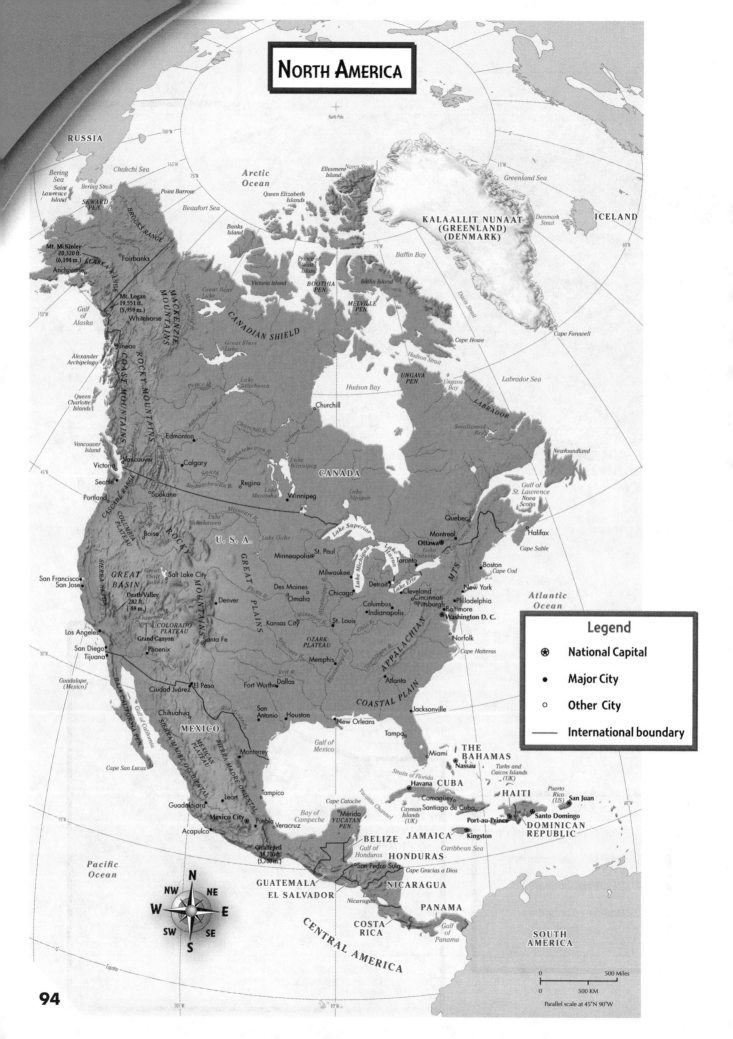

NORTH AMERICA

RUSSIA

Bering Sea
Saint Lawrence Island

Chukchi Sea

Arctic Ocean

North Pole

Ellesmere Island

Nares Strait

Greenland Sea

ICELAND

Denmark Strait

KALAALLIT NUNAAT
(GREENLAND)
(DENMARK)

Bering Strait

Point Barrow

Beaufort Sea

Queen Elizabeth Islands

SEWARD PEN.

Mt. McKinley
20,320 ft.
(6,194 m.)

°Fairbanks

ALASKA RANGE

Banks Island

Victoria Island

Prince of Wales Island

BOOTHIA PEN.

Baffin Island

Baffin Bay

Cape Howe

Cape Farewell

Anchorage

BROOKS RANGE

Gulf of Alaska

Mt. Logan
19,551 ft.
(5,959 m.)

°Whitehorse

Juneau

MACKENZIE MOUNTAINS

Great Bear Lake

MELVILLE PEN.

Davis Strait

Alexander Archipelago

COAST MOUNTAINS

ROCKY MOUNTAINS

CANADIAN SHIELD

Great Slave Lake

Hudson Strait

Labrador Sea

Queen Charlotte Islands

Peace R.

Lake Athabasca

UNGAVA PEN.

Ungava Bay

LABRADOR

Vancouver Island

Edmonton

Athabasca R.

Churchill

Churchill R.

Nelson R.

Smallwood Res.

Newfoundland

Vancouver

Victoria

Calgary

South Saskatchewan R.

North Saskatchewan R.

CANADA

Lake Winnipeg

Hudson Bay

Seattle

Regina

Lake Manitoba

Lake Nipigon

Quebec

Gulf of St. Lawrence
Nova Scotia

Portland

Spokane

Winnipeg

Lake Superior

Montreal

Halifax

CASCADE RANGE

Boise

Snake R.

Missouri R.

Lake Oahe

Ottawa ⊛

Cape Sable

COLUMBIA PLATEAU

ROCKY MOUNTAINS

Minneapolis

St. Paul

Lake Michigan

Lake Huron

Lake Ontario

Toronto

Boston

Cape Cod

San Francisco
San Jose

GREAT BASIN

Great Salt Lake

Salt Lake City

U.S.A.

GREAT PLAINS

Milwaukee

Detroit

Lake Erie

Cleveland

New York

Death Valley
-282 ft.
(-89 m.)

SIERRA NEVADA

Denver

Des Moines

Omaha

Chicago

Columbus

Cincinnati

Pittsburgh

Philadelphia

Baltimore

Atlantic Ocean

Los Angeles

COLORADO PLATEAU

Grand Canyon

Platte R.

Kansas City

St. Louis

Indianapolis

Ohio R.

Washington D. C.

APPALACHIAN MTS.

San Diego

Phoenix

Santa Fe

OZARK PLATEAU

Arkansas R.

Norfolk

Cape Hatteras

Tijuana

Guadalupe
(Mexico)

El Paso

Memphis

Red R.

Mississippi R.

Tennessee R.

Atlanta

COASTAL PLAIN

Ciudad Juárez

Fort Worth

Dallas

Jacksonville

Chihuahua

Rio Grande

San Antonio

Houston

New Orleans

BAJA CALIFORNIA PEN.

Cape San Lucas

MEXICO

SIERRA MADRE OCCIDENTAL

MEXICAN PLATEAU

Monterrey

Gulf of Mexico

Tampa

Miami

THE
BAHAMAS

Nassau

Turks and Caicos Islands (UK)

Puerto Rico
(US)

San Juan

Gulf of California

León

Tampico

Cape Catoche

Straits of Florida

Havana

CUBA

Camagüey

Cayman Islands (UK)

Santiago de Cuba

HAITI

Santo Domingo

Guadalajara

SIERRA MADRE ORIENTAL

Bay of Campeche

°Mérida

YUCATAN PEN.

Port-au-Prince

Kingston

DOMINICAN REPUBLIC

Mexico City ⊛

Puebla

Veracruz

Yucatan Channel

Acapulco

Citlaltépetl
18,700 ft.
(5,700 m.)

BELIZE

JAMAICA

Gulf of Honduras

Caribbean Sea

Pacific Ocean

HONDURAS

San Pedro Sula

Cape Gracias a Dios

GUATEMALA
EL SALVADOR

Lake Nicaragua

NICARAGUA

PANAMA

COSTA RICA

Gulf of Panama

SOUTH AMERICA

CENTRAL AMERICA

Equator

Legend

⊛   National Capital

●   Major City

○   Other City

—   International boundary

N
NW   NE
W   E
SW   SE
S

0   500 Miles
0   500 KM

Parallel scale at 45°N 90°W

THE UNITED STATES

95

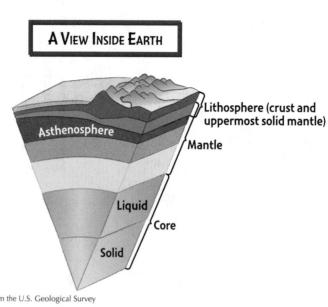

SOURCE: Based on information from the U.S. Geological Survey

Characteristics of Civilizations

Human beings lived together long before civilizations arose. A civilization will have most of the following characteristics:

- Relatively sophisticated agricultural techniques that allow farmers to grow more food than is needed to just survive.

- Large numbers of people who are able to work at jobs other than farming. This division of labor permits people to focus on other things such as science, religion, or art. This allows for the development of new technologies.

- Some type of social organization—families, chiefs, states, and/or governments.

- The gathering of people into permanent settlements, and the establishment of formal social institutions, such as places of worship, schools, and courts.

- More complicated economies, including expanded trade and a monetary (money) system, and the amassing of more material possessions than in simpler societies.

Excerpts from the Code of Hammurabi

If a judge tries a case, reaches a decision, and presents his judgment in writing; if later error shall appear in his decision, and it be through his own fault, then he shall pay twelve times the fine set by him in the case, and he shall be publicly removed from the judge's bench forever.

If anyone receives into his house a runaway male or female slave of the court, or of a freedman, and does not bring it out at the public proclamation of the major domus, the master of the house shall be put to death.

If anyone finds runaway male or female slaves in the open country and brings them to their masters, the master of the slaves shall pay him two shekels of silver.

If anyone is caught committing a robbery, then he shall be put to death. If the robber is not caught, then shall he who was robbed claim under oath the amount of his loss; then shall the community . . . on whose ground and territory and in whose domain it was compensate him for the goods stolen.

If anyone takes over a field to till it and obtains no harvest, it must be proved that he did no work on the field, and he must deliver grain, just as his neighbor raised, to the owner of the field.

If anyone opens his ditches to water his crop, but is careless, and the water floods the field of his neighbor, then he shall pay his neighbor corn for his loss.

If any man, without the knowledge of the owner of a garden, fells a tree in a garden he shall pay half a mina in money.

If a man wishes to separate from a woman or wife who has borne him children, then he shall give that wife her dowry and a right to use some of the field, garden, and property, so that she can rear her children. When she has brought up her children, a portion of all that is given to the children, equal as that of one son, shall be given to her. She may then marry the man of her heart.

If a man wishes to separate from his wife who has borne him no children, he shall give her the amount of her purchase money and the dowry she brought from her father's house, and let her go.

If a woman quarrels with her husband and says, "You are not pleasant to me," the reasons for her prejudice must be presented. If she is guiltless, and there is no fault on her part, but he leaves and neglects her, then no guilt attaches to this woman; she shall take her dowry and go back to her father's house.

If a son strikes his father, his hands shall be hewn off. If a man puts out the eye of another man, his eye shall be put out. If he breaks another man's bone, his bone shall be broken.

If a man strikes a free-born woman so that she loses her unborn child, he shall pay ten shekels for her loss. If the woman dies, his daughter shall be put to death.

If a builder builds a house for someone, and does not construct it properly, and the house falls in and kills its owner, then that builder shall be put to death. If it kills the son of the owner, the son of that builder shall be put to death.

If a slave say to his master: "You are not my master," if they convict him his master shall cut off his ear.

The Dynasties of China

Dynasty	Dates	Major Events
Xia	*2205–1570 B.C.	Agriculture, bronze, first writing
Shang or Yin	*1570–1045 B.C.	First major dynasty; first Chinese calendar, metallurgy, uniform writing code
Zhou	*1045–256 B.C.	Developed society using money, iron, written laws; age of Confucius
Qin	221–206 B.C.	Unification after period of Warring States; building of Great Wall begun; road building
Han	206 B.C.–A.D. 220	First centralized and effectively administered empire; introduction of Buddhism
Three Kingdoms Period	220–265	Division into three states: prolonged fighting and eventual victory of the state of Wei over Chu and Wu
Jin	265–317	Beginning of Hun invasions in the north
Sui	581–618	Reunification; barbarian invasions stopped; Great Wall refortified
Tang	618–907	Centralized government; empire greatly extended; period of excellence in sculpture, painting, and poetry
Wu Dai (Five Dynasties)	907–959	Economic depression and loss of territory in northern China, central Asia, and Korea; first use of paper money
Song	960–1279	Period of calm and creativity; printing developed (movable type); central government restored; northern and western frontiers neglected and Mongol invasions began
Yuan	1279–1368	Beginning of Mongol rule in China, under Kublai Khan; time of Marco Polo's visit; dynasty brought to an end by revolts
Ming	1368–1644	Mongols driven out by native Chinese; Mongolia captured by second Ming emperor; period of architectural development; Beijing flourished as new capital; refortification of Great Wall
Qing (Manchu)	1644–1911	China once again under non-Chinese rule; the Qing conquered by nomads from Manchuria; trade with the West; culture flourished, but the dynasty was overthrown by nationalistic revolutionaries

*Dates are approximate.

Major Religions of the World

	Origins and History	Number of Believers	Belief about God	Purpose of Life	Belief about Afterlife	Holy Texts
Buddhism	Founded by Siddhartha Gautama (the Buddha) 520 B.C., in Northeast India	360 million	Varies: Theravada is atheistic; Mahayana has many deities. Buddha taught that nothing is permanent.	Purpose is to avoid suffering and gain enlightenment and release from the cycle of rebirth, or at least attain a better rebirth by gaining merit.	Reincarnation until enlightenment is gained	Tripitaka (Pali Canon); Mahayana sutras like the Lotus Sutra; others
Christianity	Founded by Jesus of Nazareth A.D. 30, near Jerusalem	2 billion	One God, who is a Trinity of Father, Son, and Holy Spirit	All are separated from God because of sin. Salvation is through faith in Jesus (and, for some, sacraments and good works).	Eternal heaven or hell or temporary purgatory	The Holy Bible (Old and New Testaments)
Hinduism	Local religion of India as developed to present day	900 million	One Supreme Reality (Brahman) shown in many deities	Human beings are slaves to ignorance and illusion, but can escape. Purpose is to gain release from rebirth, or at least a better rebirth.	Reincarnation until enlightenment is gained	The Vedas, Upanishads, Bhagavad Gita, Ramayana
Islam	Founded by Muhammad in A.D. 622, in Arabia	1.3 billion (Sunni: 940 million)	One God, called *Allah*	Human beings must submit (Islam) to Allah's will to gain paradise after death.	Paradise or hell	Quran (Scripture); Hadith (tradition)
Judaism	The religion of the Hebrews in Israel (1300 B.C.), especially after the destruction of the Second Temple in Jerusalem, A.D. 70	14 million	One God, called *Yahweh*	Obey God's commandments, live ethically. More a focus on this life than afterlife.	Not historically emphasized; beliefs vary from no afterlife to shadowy existence to the "World to Come" (similar to heaven)	Bible (Tanakh), Talmud

World War II in Europe: 20 Selected Key Events

Event	Date
1. Mussolini comes to power in Italy.	October 31, 1922
2. Adolf Hitler becomes new Chancellor of Germany.	January 30, 1933
3. Ethiopia surrenders to Italian forces.	May 1936
4. Italy and Germany form Rome-Berlin Axis.	November 1, 1937
5. German troops annex Austria.	March 12, 1938
6. Munich Agreement sacrifices Czechoslovakia to Hitler.	September 29, 1938
7. Germany invades and conquers Poland.	September 1939
8. Winston Churchill becomes new Prime Minister of Britain.	May 10, 1940
9. France surrenders to Germany.	June 1940
10. Battle of Britain (German air raids on British Isles)	July to October, 1940
11. Germany invades Soviet Union.	June 22, 1941
12. Germany and Italy declare war on U.S.	December 11, 1941
13. British defeat Germans at El Alamein.	July 2, 1942
14. Battle of Stalingrad	August 1942 to February 1943
15. Allies invade Sicily.	July 10, 1943
16. Allies land on Italian mainland.	September 3, 1943
17. Allies invade Normandy.	June 6, 1944
18. Liberation of Paris	August 1944
19. Allies defeat Germans at the Battle of the Bulge.	December 27, 1944
20. Germany surrenders to the Allies.	May 7, 1945

Dates of Independence for Former Soviet Republics

Former Soviet Republic	Date of Independence
Lithuania	March 11, 1990
Georgia	April 9, 1991
Estonia	August 20, 1991
Latvia	August 21, 1991
Belarus	August 25, 1991
Moldova	August 27, 1991
Azerbaijan	August 30, 1991
Uzbekistan	August 29, 1991
Kyrgyzstan	August 31, 1991
Tajikistan	September 9, 1991
Armenia	September 23, 1991
Turkmenistan	October 27, 1991
Kazakhstan	December 16, 1991
Russia	December 26, 1991
Ukraine	December 26, 1991

Ecoregions of the World

Tropical Rainforest	Dominated by wide variety of mostly evergreen trees forming a closed canopy with little light reaching the ground; abundant rainfall, brief dry season
Tropical Deciduous Forest	Similar to tropical rainforest, but rainy and dry seasons are more distinct; usually less rainfall; sometimes prominent thorny vegetation
Tropical Scrub	Similar to tropical deciduous forest, but mostly smaller trees; prolonged dry season; many thorny plants can be found here
Tropical Savanna	Grasslands with scattered individual trees that do not form a closed canopy
Desert	Typically sparse vegetation, low and unpredictable rainfall; daily temperatures typically fluctuate
Mediterranean	Found in coastal areas between 30 and 40 degrees latitude; dominated by stands of dense, spiny shrubs with tough evergreen leaves
Grassland	Areas dominated by grasses, such as prairies or meadows
Temperate Broadleaf Forest	Dominated by deciduous trees; moderate to large seasonal changes in temperature; evenly distributed rainfall
Boreal Forest or Taiga	Dominated by coniferous trees; long, cold winters and short, wet summers; few tree species
Tundra	Low, shrubby, or mat-like vegetation; soils usually subject to permafrost; low plant diversity, short growing season
Polar or Mountain Summits	Summits of high mountains, either without vegetation or covered by low, tundra-like vegetation; also includes bodies of land ice

Understanding Latitude and Longitude

The **equator** is an imaginary line drawn around the center of Earth. More lines are drawn parallel to the equator. These are called lines (or parallels) of latitude. The latitude of any place on Earth is its distance north or south of the equator, measured in degrees. The equator is 0°. The latitude of the North Pole is 90°N (this is read as "ninety degrees north"). The latitude of the South Pole is 90°S ("ninety degrees south").

The prime meridian is an imaginary line around Earth from the North Pole to the South Pole that runs through the city of Greenwich, England. Other lines drawn parallel to the prime meridian are called lines (or meridians) of longitude. Like latitude, longitude is measured in degrees. The longitude of New York City is 74°W ("seventy-four degrees west").

The equator divides Earth into the Northern and Southern Hemispheres. The prime meridian divides Earth into the Western and Eastern Hemispheres. Hemisphere means *half of a globe*.

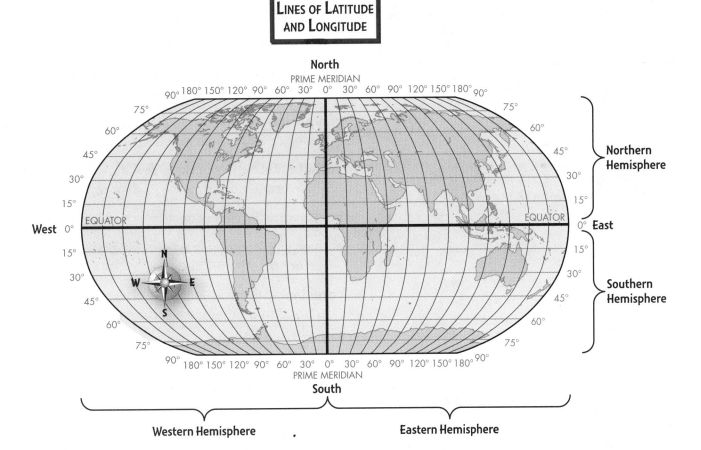

Glossary

A

Abbasid Dynasty: Islamic dynasty created by Abu al-Abbas in 750

acropolis: a fortified hill of ancient Greece

agora: an open space that served as a market, a religious center, and gathering place in ancient Greece

anthropologist: a scientist who studies human beings and their ancestors

archaeologist: a scientist who studies fossils and other remains of human cultures

artifacts: items that ancient people left behind that are studied by scientists to learn about ancient societies

assembly: political body that passed the laws in ancient Greece

asthenosphere: the soft area of inner Earth that lies beneath the lithosphere

B

Berlin Conference: meeting of competing European powers in 1884 to develop guidelines for colonizing Africa

biodiversity: the variety of plant and animal species living in a certain area

boundaries: the edges of tectonic plates

Brezhnev Doctrine: the Soviet policy of putting down dissident movements with military force

C

city-states: form of government with cities that act as independent states

climate: the usual pattern of weather in a particular place, including precipitation

Cold War: political tensions that resulted from the division of Europe between the Soviet Union and western powers following World War II

colonialism: sending citizens to a distant territory to gain control over its economy and politics

coniferous trees: trees that produce cones and needles rather than leaves

conquistadors: Spanish explorers who sought power and riches in the Americas

consuls: men who ran the army and government during the Roman republic

continent: a large landmass

convergent boundary: where one plate pushes underneath another

core: inner region of Earth that consists of a hot liquid outer core and a solid inner core

crust: the thin, outer shell of Earth

cuneiform: system of writing developed by the ancient Sumerians

D

D-Day: June 6, 1944, the first day of the invasion of Normandy by the Allied powers

deciduous trees: trees, such as maple trees, that usually lose their leaves at some time during the year

Delian League: Athens and its allies during the Peloponnesian War with Sparta

deoxyribonucleic acid (DNA): taken by scientists from ancient fossils; contains the genetic code for all human life

divergent boundary: where plates pull away from one another

E

earthquakes: a shaking of Earth due to the readjustment of Earth's surface because of plate movement

ecoregion: an area of land or water that has a collection of plants and animals that is unique to that area

elevation: the height of the land usually in relation to sea level

empire: a state that rules a large territory and population and is controlled by a single leader called an emperor

endangered: plants or animals that are threatened or in danger of dying out

ephors: a group of five men in ancient Spartan society who were elected annually to be in charge of education

equator: an imaginary line drawn around the center of Earth

excavation: area where archaeologists dig

F

Fertile Crescent: also called *Mesopotamia,* this was the location of the first known civilization that developed around 3500 B.C. at Sumer

First Triumvirate: three powerful generals, Crassus, Julius Caesar, and Pompey, who shared equal rule of Rome in 60 B.C.

Five Pillars of Islam: methods of Islamic worship written in the Quran

food web: the interdependent relationship of organisms in an ecosystem

fossil fuels: fuels, such as oil, coal, and natural gas, created in Earth from the ancient remains of plants and animals

fossils: human bones from ancient cultures

G

Genghis Khan: or *universal ruler,* was the leader Temujin who unified the Mongols in 1206 and established the Mongol empire

geography: the study of Earth in all its variety

geologist: scientist who studies Earth to develop theories that try to explain its processes

H

habitat: the place where plants and animals live

hajj: religious pilgrimage

helots: people captured by the Spartans of ancient Greece and forced to work for them

Hijrah: Muhammad's journey from Mecca to Medina in the year 622

Homo erectus: a type of ancient human being who migrated out of Africa and eventually died out or evolved to be part of *homo sapiens*

Homo sapiens: early human beings who originated in central east Africa about 100,000–200,000 years ago

Homo sapiens neanderthalensis (Neanderthals): a type of ancient human being who migrated out of Africa and eventually died out

imperator: title of chief commander first bestowed by the Roman senate on Augustus in 27 B.C.

intra-plate volcanoes: volcanoes that are not located along tectonic plate boundaries

invasive species: plants or animals that have been introduced to an area where they do not occur naturally and have a negative effect on native species

Iron Curtain: term used to describe the isolated Soviet satellite states of eastern Europe during the Cold War

Islam: religion of Muslims based on the Quran and the teachings of Muhammad and his followers

isthmus: a narrow bridge of land linking two larger land masses

Kaaba: important shrine of Islam in the city of Mecca

khanates: the four territorial divisions of the Mongol empire after the death of Genghis Khan

Kublai Khan: the grandson of Genghis Khan who established the Yuan, or Mongol, Dynasty in China in 1279

Law of Nations: laws of Rome that applied to all people

legend: an area on a map that explains what each symbol on the map means

lithosphere: the outer portion of the surface of Earth that is composed of the crust and part of the mantle and consists of many large, separate plates

lock: an enclosed part of a canal in which the water level can be raised or lowered to allow for ship traffic between bodies of water with different elevations

magma: hot, liquid rock that erupts through Earth's surface, usually from a volcano

mantle: the area beneath Earth's crust that is thick and hot and is partly made of liquid rock

Mesopotamia: also called the *Fertile Crescent*, this was the location of the first known civilization that developed around 3500 B.C. at Sumer

migrate: the process of moving permanently from one place to another

Muslims: people who practice the religion of Islam

nonrenewable energy: sources of energy that will eventually be used up

North Atlantic Treaty Organization (NATO): a 1949 alliance for mutual defense against the Soviet bloc countries between the United States and some Western European nations

ocean tide: the rise and fall of the ocean due to the gravity of the moon and the sun

oil consumption: the amount of oil that a country uses over a certain period of time

oil reserves: the estimated amount of oil a country could take from the ground in the future

Operation Overlord: code name for the invasion of Normandy by Allied powers in June of 1944

organism: a living thing; usually a plant or animal

patricians: wealthy landowners within Roman society

Pax Mongolica: or *Mongol Peace,* was the period of strong and stable rule of the Mongol empire

Pax Romana: or *Roman Peace,* was the period from about 27 B.C. to A.D. 180 when the Roman empire was mostly free from civil war

Peloponnesian League: Sparta and its allies during the Peloponnesian War with Athens and its allies

Peloponnesian War: war between ancient Athens and Sparta and their allies that began in 431 B.C. and lasted for 27 years

perennial sea ice: ice of the Arctic that remains frozen all year

perestroika: a policy of restructuring the Soviet economic system to a market economy

plate-boundary volcano: a type of volcano that forms along the boundaries of Earth's shifting plates

plebeians: smaller landowners, craftsmen, and traders within Roman society

polis: the city-state, or government, of ancient Greece

praetor: person in charge of the law that applied to Roman citizens during the time of the republic

quipu: a system of knotted strings for recordkeeping used in the Inca society of South America

Quran: the holy book of Islam

radiocarbon dating: a scientific method of determining the age of artifacts and fossils

renewable energy: sources that can keep producing energy indefinitely without being used up

republic: a form of government in which leaders are elected into power by the people

Roman Confederation: organization through which early Rome ruled the Italian peninsula

S

Second Triumvirate: the rule of Rome by three generals, Octavian, Antony, and Lepidus, that began in 43 B.C.

senate: a powerful political body of the Roman republic consisting of wealthy landowners and people's assemblies

Shariah: Islamic code of law

Shiite: Islamic group loyal to Hussein, Muhammad's grandson

Silk Road: ancient trade routes across Asia

site grid: a method of dividing up the area of an archaeological excavation with stakes and string

subduction: tectonic plates of Earth forced under one another which may result in deep trenches or mountain ranges

successor: next person to rule

Sumer: the earliest of all civilizations; developed in Mesopotamia around 3500 B.C.

Sunni: Islamic group loyal to the Umayyads

T

technology: the level of knowledge of an ancient people as evidenced by their tools, shelter, or other creations

tectonic plates: large plates of the lithosphere that move very slowly upon the partly molten rock of the asthenosphere

theory: an idea of how something may have happened

transform boundary: where plates slide past one another.

Treaty of Tordesillas (1494): treaty between Spain and Portugal providing rules for colonizing Asia and the Americas

trenches: deep areas beneath the ocean formed by the movement of tectonic plates

U

Umayyad dynasty: Islamic dynasty created in 661 by Muawiyah

V

volcanoes: mountains where magma (hot, liquid rock) may erupt through Earth's surface due to the movement of tectonic plates

W

Warsaw Pact: a 1955 alliance between the Soviet Union and some countries of eastern Europe in response to the formation of the North Atlantic Treaty Organization (NATO)

Y

Yuan, or Mongol Dynasty: Chinese dynasty established in 1279 by Kublai Khan, a grandson of Genghis Khan

Z

ziggurat: ancient Sumerian temple

Index

A

Abbasid dynasty, 40
Abu al-Abbas, 40
Abu Bakr, 40
acropolis, 21
adaptation of organisms to environment, 74, 78–79
Africa, colonialism in, 44–49
African independence dates, 48–49
agora, 21
air pollution, 81
Akkadians, 15
Allah, 38–39, 43
Allied powers, 62
Americas, Spanish explorers in, 50–51, 54–55
anthropologists, 2–3
Antony, 27
Anu, 15
aquatic ecoregions, 74
Arabian Peninsula, 38–39
archaeological sites, 2, 6–7
archaeologists, 2–3
Arctic, 86–91
Arctic Circle, 86, 88–89
Arctic Ocean, 86, 88–89, 91
Aristotle, 21
artifacts, 2–3, 7
assembly, 21
asthenosphere, 8, 12, 96
Atahualpa, 51
Athens, 21–25
Augustus, 26–27
Aurelius, Marcus, 28
Aztec empire, 50–51

B

Babylonian kingdom, 16–17
Baghdad, 40
Balboa, 51
beachheads, 64
benthic realm, 91
Beringia, 4
Bering Strait, 86
Berlin Conference, 44, 48
biodiversity, 75, 78
biological realms, 91
boreal forest, 75, 77, 102

boundaries of tectonic plates, 8–13
Bradley, Omar, 63
Brezhnev, Leonid, 68
Brezhnev Doctrine, 68, 72
Buddhism, 43, 99

C

Caesar, Julius, 27
caliph, 40
capital, 44
caravan, 38–39
Carter, Jimmy, 58
casualties, 64
Challenger Deep, 10–11
Chinese dynasties, 32–33, 36–37, 98
Chinese inventions, 36–37
Christianity, 43, 99
CIS (Commonwealth of Independent States), 70–71
city-states, 15
civilizations, characteristics of, 18–19, 96
civil war, 27
climate, 74
coal, 80–81, 87
Code of Hammurabi, 15, 19, 97
Cold War, 68–69, 72
colonialism, 44
colonialism in Africa, 44–49
Columbus, Christopher, 50–51
combustion, 80
Commonwealth of Independent States (CIS), 70–71
Congo, 44
coniferous trees, 76, 102
conquistadors, 50
conservation plan, 75
consuls, 26
convergent boundary, 9
core, of Earth, 8, 96
Coronado, 51
Cortés, Hernán, 50–51
Cradle of Civilization, 16
Crassus, 27
crust, of Earth, 8, 96
Culebra Cut, 57
culture
    Greek, 24–25
    Roman, 30–31
cuneiform, 15
Cuzco, 51–53

volcanoes, 9–11

Warsaw Pact, 68–69, 72
wind power, 80, 85
world map, 92–93
World War II
    key events, 100
    Normandy invasion, 62–67, 100
Wu Dai Dynasty, 98

Xia Dynasty, 98

Yin Dynasty, 98
Yuan Dynasty, 32–33, 98

Zakat, 43
Zhou Dynasty, 98
Zhu Yuanzhang, 33
ziggurats, 15–16

Answer Key

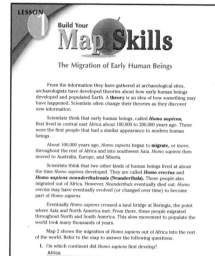

LESSON 1

Build Your Map Skills

The Migration of Early Human Beings

From the information they have gathered at archaeological sites, archaeologists have developed theories about how early human beings developed and populated Earth. A **theory** is an idea of how something may have happened. Scientists often change their theories as they discover new information.

Scientists think that early human beings, called *Homo sapiens,* first lived in central east Africa about 100,000 to 200,000 years ago. These were the first people that had a similar appearance to modern human beings.

About 100,000 years ago, *Homo sapiens* began to **migrate**, or move, throughout the rest of Africa and into southwest Asia. *Homo sapiens* then moved to Australia, Europe, and Siberia.

Scientists think that two other kinds of human beings lived at about the time *Homo sapiens* developed. They are called *Homo erectus* and *Homo sapiens neanderthalensis* (**Neanderthals**). These people also migrated out of Africa. However, *Neanderthals* eventually died out. *Homo erectus* may have eventually evolved (or changed over time) to become part of *Homo sapiens.*

Eventually *Homo sapiens* crossed a land bridge at Beringia, the point where Asia and North America met. From there, these people migrated throughout North and South America. This slow movement to populate the world took many thousands of years.

Map 2 shows the migration of *Homo sapiens* out of Africa into the rest of the world. Refer to the map to answer the following questions.

1. On which continent did *Homo sapiens* first develop?
   Africa

4

---

2. Which parts of North and South America were populated by water routes? Land routes?
   The northwest, central, and eastern regions of North America were populated via land routes. This is also true for most of Central America and the interior of South America. The extreme west coasts of both continents were populated via water routes.

3. Which region on the map was the first to be populated by *Homo sapiens* after they left Africa? Which was the last? Explain when *Homo sapiens* first migrated into these areas.
   First: southwest Asia (100,000 years ago); last: Chile (13,000 years ago).

4. Use the compass rose to describe the migration range of *Homo erectus.*
   ***Homo erectus* lived in east central Africa, southwest Asia, parts of southeast Asia, and a small part of the northwest coast of Africa.**

5. Which regions on the map were home to *Homo sapiens neanderthalensis*?
   central and southern Europe and southwest Asia

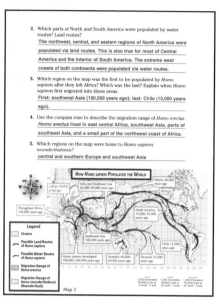

5

LESSON 1

More about Early Human Beings

Something to Think About

Why is it important to learn about early human beings?

Use the information from pages 2–3 and the map on page 5 to answer questions 1–6. For question 7, you will need to do some library research on your own.

1. Use Map 2 on page 5 to create a timeline showing which continents were populated by *Homo sapiens* and when.

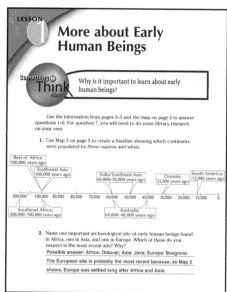

2. Name one important archaeological site of early human beings found in Africa, one in Asia, and one in Europe. Which of these do you suspect is the most recent site? Why?
   Possible answer: Africa: Olduvai; Asia: Java; Europe: Boxgrove.
   The European site is probably the most recent because, as Map 2 shows, Europe was settled long after Africa and Asia.

6

---

3. North and South America are separated by water from the other continents. How did *Homo sapiens* migrate to the Americas?
   Though the Americas are separated today by water from the other continents, that was not always the case. Thousands of years ago, a land bridge in the region known as Beringia connected northeastern Asia (Siberia) with North America. *Homo sapiens* were able to use the land bridge to move between continents.

4. Name two other kinds of human beings that lived at about the same time that *Homo sapiens* began to develop. What happened to these groups?
   Homo erectus* and *Homo sapiens neanderthalensis* (Neanderthals) lived at the same time as *Homo sapiens.* Neanderthals eventually died out, but *Homo erectus* may have eventually evolved to become part of *Homo sapiens.

5. Why is it important for scientists to keep track of the different levels in the ground where artifacts at archaeological sites are found?
   This is important because artifacts at a higher level within the ground are usually more recent than those at a lower level.

6. How can scientists determine the kinds of foods *Homo sapiens* ate?
   Plant remains and animal bones found at archaeological sites indicate the types of food eaten by ancient people.

7. Do some library research to form a theory about why *Homo sapiens* were able to be so successful. Write your ideas on the lines below. Provide evidence for your theory.
   Possible answer: The expansion of the brain cavity and brain was important in allowing *Homo sapiens* to learn. In addition, the development of walking upright on two legs allowed *Homo sapiens* to travel and hunt more easily. The evolution of the larynx and hyoid bone, which made speech possible, was also important in allowing *Homo sapiens* to communicate.

7

LESSON 2

Build Your Map Skills

The Ring of Fire

Geologists' theory of plate tectonics explains the location of volcanoes. Volcanoes tend to form along the boundaries of Earth's shifting plates: the edges of continents, undersea mountain ranges, or chains of islands. These types of volcanoes are called **plate-boundary volcanoes.**

Mt. St. Helens, Mt. Hood, and Mt. Rainier in the Cascade Range in the northwest United States are plate-boundary volcanoes. The Cascade volcanoes were formed by the Juan de Fuca plate being forced underneath the North American plate.

Some volcanoes are not located along plate boundaries. These are called **intra-plate volcanoes.** Geologists think that these form at a "hot spot" within a plate where magma is forced to Earth's surface. The Hawaiian islands comprise a volcanic chain of islands with intra-plate volcanoes.

Magma is being forced to the surface of this volcano.

Many of the most active volcanoes in the world are in the Pacific Ocean area. Because so many volcanoes are concentrated there, the area is often referred to as the *Ring of Fire.*

One of the deepest places in the ocean was made from the collision of two tectonic plates. This location is called *Challenger Deep* (see the map).

Refer to the map on the next page to answer the following questions.

1. Which tectonic plate does most of the United States sit on?
   the North American Plate

10

---

2. Which trench within the Ring of Fire lies farthest north? Which lies farthest west?
   Farthest north: the Aleutian Trench; farthest west: the Java Trench

3. Describe the location of Challenger Deep. It lies near which trench?
   Challenger Deep lies in the western Pacific Ocean, just north of the equator at the southern end of the Marianas Trench.

4. What underwater ridge has formed where the North and South American plates meet the African and Eurasian plates?
   the Mid-Atlantic Ridge

5. Use the compass rose to help describe three of the plates that border the Pacific Plate along the Ring of Fire.
   Possible answer: The Australian Plate borders the Pacific Plate to the southwest; the Philippine Plate borders it to the northwest; and the North American Plate borders it to the northwest, north, and east.

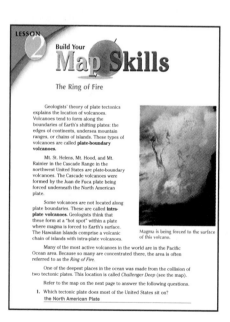

11

Answer Key

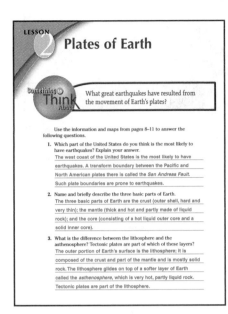

LESSON 2 — Plates of Earth

Think About: What great earthquakes have resulted from the movement of Earth's plates?

Use the information and maps from pages 8–11 to answer the following questions.

1. Which part of the United States do you think is the most likely to have earthquakes? Explain your answer.
   The west coast of the United States is the most likely to have earthquakes. A transform boundary between the Pacific and North American plates there is called the *San Andreas Fault*. Such plate boundaries are prone to earthquakes.

2. Name and briefly describe the three basic parts of Earth.
   The three basic parts of Earth are the crust (outer shell, hard and very thin); the mantle (thick and hot and partly made of liquid rock); and the core (consisting of a hot liquid outer core and a solid inner core).

3. What is the difference between the lithosphere and the asthenosphere? Tectonic plates are part of which of these layers?
   The outer portion of Earth's surface is the lithosphere; it is composed of the crust and part of the mantle and is mostly solid rock. The lithosphere glides on top of a softer layer of Earth called the *asthenosphere*, which is very hot, partly liquid rock. Tectonic plates are part of the lithosphere.

12

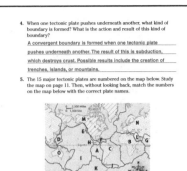

4. When one tectonic plate pushes underneath another, what kind of boundary is formed? What is the action and result of this kind of boundary?
   A convergent boundary is formed when one tectonic plate pushes underneath another. The result of this is subduction, which destroys crust. Possible results include the creation of trenches, islands, or mountains.

5. The 15 major tectonic plates are numbered on the map below. Study the map on page 11. Then, without looking back, match the numbers on the map below with the correct plate names.

1. F	Caribbean Plate	9. K	Antarctic Plate
2. E	Juan de Fuca Plate	10. A	Nazca Plate
3. N	Eurasian Plate	11. M	North American Plate
4. G	Indian Plate	12. I	Pacific Plate
5. L	Arabian Plate	13. C	South American Plate
6. B	African Plate	14. D	Philippine Plate
7. O	Australian Plate	15. H	Cocos Plate
8. J	Scotia Plate		

13

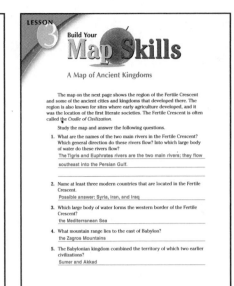

LESSON 3 — Build Your Map Skills

A Map of Ancient Kingdoms

The map on the next page shows the region of the Fertile Crescent and some of the ancient cities and kingdoms that developed there. The region is also known for sites where early agriculture developed, and it was the location of the first literate societies. The Fertile Crescent is often called the *Cradle of Civilization*.

Study the map and answer the following questions.

1. What are the names of the two main rivers in the Fertile Crescent? Which general direction do these rivers flow? Into which large body of water do these rivers flow?
   The Tigris and Euphrates rivers are the two main rivers; they flow southeast into the Persian Gulf.

2. Name at least three modern countries that are located in the Fertile Crescent.
   Possible answer: Syria, Iran, and Iraq

3. Which large body of water forms the western border of the Fertile Crescent?
   the Mediterranean Sea

4. What mountain range lies to the east of Babylon?
   the Zagros Mountains

5. The Babylonian kingdom combined the territory of which two earlier civilizations?
   Sumer and Akkad

16

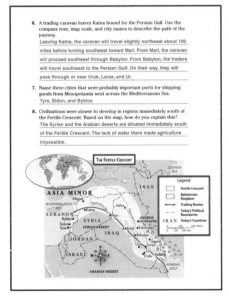

6. A trading caravan leaves Katna bound for the Persian Gulf. Use the compass rose, map scale, and city names to describe the path of the journey.
   Leaving Katna, the caravan will travel slightly northeast about 100 miles before turning southeast toward Mari. From Mari, the caravan will proceed southeast through Babylon. From Babylon, the traders will travel southeast to the Persian Gulf. On their way, they will pass through or near Uruk, Larsa, and Ur.

7. Name three cities that were probably important ports for shipping goods from Mesopotamia west across the Mediterranean Sea.
   Tyre, Sidon, and Byblos.

8. Civilizations were slower to develop in regions immediately south of the Fertile Crescent. Based on the map, how do you explain this?
   The Syrian and the Arabian deserts are situated immediately south of the Fertile Crescent. The lack of water there made agriculture impossible.

17

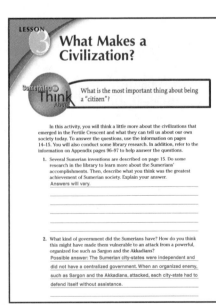

LESSON 3 — What Makes a Civilization?

Think About: What is the most important thing about being a "citizen"?

In this activity, you will think a little more about the civilizations that emerged in the Fertile Crescent and what they can tell us about our own society today. To answer the questions, use the information on pages 14–15. You will also conduct some library research. In addition, refer to the information on Appendix pages 96–97 to help answer the questions.

1. Several Sumerian inventions are described on page 15. Do some research in the library to learn more about the Sumerians' accomplishments. Then, describe what you think was the greatest achievement of Sumerian society. Explain your answer.
   Answers will vary.

2. What kind of government did the Sumerians have? How do you think this might have made them vulnerable to an attack from a powerful, organized foe such as Sargon and the Akkadians?
   Possible answer: The Sumerian city-states were independent and did not have a centralized government. When an organized enemy, such as Sargon and the Akkadians, attacked, each city-state had to defend itself without assistance.

18

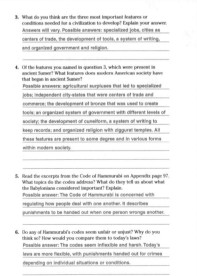

3. What do you think are the three most important features or conditions needed for a civilization to develop? Explain your answer.
   Answers will vary. Possible answers: specialized jobs, cities as centers of trade, the development of tools, a system of writing, and organized government and religion.

4. Of the features you named in question 3, which were present in ancient Sumer? What features does modern American society have that began in ancient Sumer?
   Possible answers: agricultural surpluses that led to specialized jobs; independent city-states that were centers of trade and commerce; the development of bronze that was used to create tools; an organized system of government with different levels of society; the development of cuneiform, a system of writing to keep records; and organized religion with ziggurat temples. All these features are present to some degree and in various forms within modern society.

5. Read the excerpts from the Code of Hammurabi on Appendix page 97. What topics do the codes address? What do they tell us about what the Babylonians considered important? Explain.
   Possible answer: The Code of Hammurabi is concerned with regulating how people deal with one another. It describes punishments to be handed out when one person wrongs another.

6. Do any of Hammurabi's codes seem unfair or unjust? Why or why not do you think so? How would you compare them to today's laws?
   Possible answer: The codes seem inflexible and harsh. Today's laws are more flexible, with punishments handed out for crimes depending on individual situations or conditions.

19

Answer Key

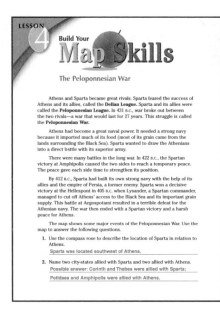

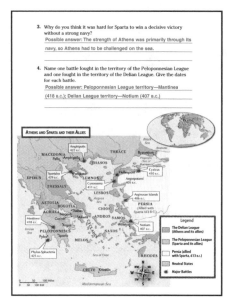

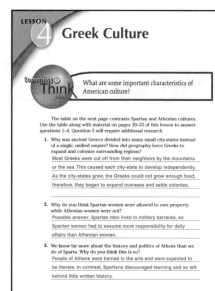

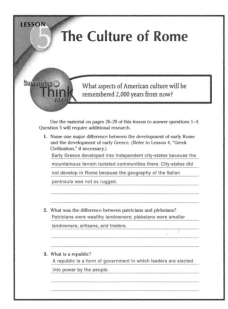

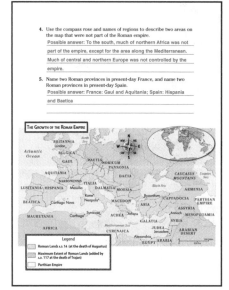

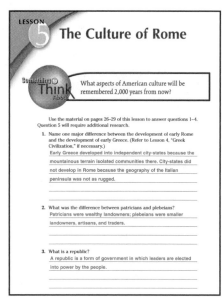

Answer Key

Page 31

4. Describe how Rome slowly changed from a republic to an empire ruled by one man.
   Possible answer: By the 100s b.c., Rome was controlled by a small number of patricians. Many small farmers lost their land because they could not compete with them. This hurt the republic's ability to recruit soldiers, who had largely come from small landowners loyal to the republic. Generals began recruiting soldiers by promising them land, but this caused the soldiers to be loyal to the generals rather than to the republic itself. Rome was engaged in civil war as various generals sought power. Finally, the First Triumvirate of generals gained power in 60 b.c. Caesar soon gained control of the government and became dictator. After his assassination and another struggle between three new generals, Augustus became emperor, thus beginning the tradition of an emperor (a single, powerful military leader) ruling Rome.

5. Select one of the topics from the list below. Do some library research to write a two-page paper on one of the following topics. Feel free to add visual aids, drawings, or photos to your report.
   - The principles of law from the Law of Nations and/or the Twelve Tables and their influence
   - A brief biography about one of the "Five Good Emperors," focusing on his main accomplishments and failures
   - The names and roles of the Roman gods and goddesses
   - A summary of the plot of Virgil's *Aeneid* or Ovid's *Metamorphoses*
   - The role of women in Roman society
   - A summary of the teachings of *Meditations*, by Marcus Aurelius
   - The characteristics of Roman art
   - A list of problems that led to the fall of the Roman empire
   - A summary of the Romulus and Remus story and what it tells about the Romans' sense of their own importance

31

Page 34

LESSON 6
Build Your Map Skills
The "Mongol Peace"

As you already learned, the Mongol empire was eventually divided into four khanates. Each went to a son of Genghis Khan. The ruler of Mongolia and China, called the *Great Khanate*, was the overlord of the entire Mongol empire.

The Mongol empire connected the eastern world with the western world. Previously these cultures had been separated because of great geographical distances and the many separate kingdoms that made travel difficult. The phrase *Pax Mongolica* (Mongol Peace) was used to describe this period of strong and stable rule.

The Mongol rulers were generally tolerant of other religions and cultures. They encouraged trade by making east-west trade routes safe for travelers. These ancient trade routes, together called the **Silk Road**, were among the earliest connections between the cultures of Europe and Asia.

Use the map to answer the following questions.

1. Which khanate occupied the northwestern region of the Mongol empire? Which khanate occupied the southwestern region of the empire? Name a principal city in each region.
   northwest: Kipchak Khanate, Moscow; southwest: Ilkhanate, Baghdad

2. Describe the water route a trader would have followed when journeying from Rome to Hangzhou. Use the compass rose to help with your description.
   The trader would have traveled to the southeast through the Mediterranean Sea to Alexandria and then southeast through the Red Sea before turning east through the Indian Ocean. The trader would have followed the southeast coast of India and southern China and turned north through the South China Sea, following the east coast of China to Hangzhou.

34

Page 35

3. Which geographical barrier might have made it difficult for the Mongols to advance south into India?
   the Himalaya Mountains

4. Into which areas south of China did the Mongol empire advance after 1240?
   Burma, Khmer, and Vietnam

5. What geographical areas did the Great Wall separate?
   It separated China from Mongolia and the Mongol empire.

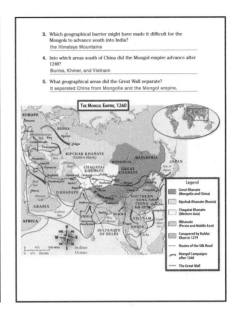

35

Page 36

LESSON 6
The Chinese Dynasties

Something to Think About
What is the most important American accomplishment of the last 25 years?

In this lesson, you learned about the Yuan Dynasty in China and how the Ming Dynasty began. Refer to the information on pages 32–35 and the table on the next page to answer more questions about China and its dynasties. You will also need to refer to Appendix page 98.

1. Identify the first major Chinese dynasty and the dates when it flourished. What major accomplishments occurred during this period?
   The Shang or Yin Dynasty (1570–1045 b.c.) was the first major dynasty. Accomplishments included the first Chinese calendar, metallurgy, and a uniform writing code.

2. Which dynasty collapsed when the Mongols invaded China?
   the Song Dynasty

3. In which dynasty did the building of the Great Wall begin? In which dynasties was the wall refortified? Why was the wall strengthened?
   Construction began during the Qin Dynasty. It was refortified during the Sui and Ming dynasties. It was probably strengthened to keep out northern invaders, such as the Mongols.

4. Which of the inventions in the graph on the next page do you think was the most important? Why?
   Students' answers will vary.

36

Page 37

5. According to the graph, when was the iron plow invented in China, and when was it first used in the West? How much time passed from the time the iron plow was invented until it was used in the West?
   The iron plow was invented in China around 300 b.c. It was used in the West about a.d. 1000—around 1,300 years later.

6. During which dynasty was paper invented in China?
   Paper was invented during the Han Dynasty.

7. When did Marco Polo visit China? Name two items in the graph he might have seen for the first time on his visit. How do you know?
   He visited China in 1275–1291. Cast iron and porcelain were probably new to him because they weren't adopted in Europe until after 1300.

8. Use the information from your own library research to write three paragraphs on a separate piece of paper about which Chinese dynasty you think was the greatest or most important. Make sure to use specific examples to justify your argument.

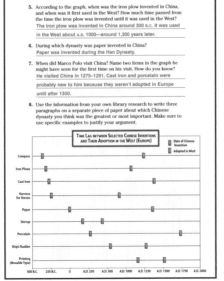

37

Page 40

LESSON 7
Build Your Map Skills
The Islamic Empire

After his death, Muhammad's followers chose Abu Bakr to be caliph, or successor. Islam soon expanded into an empire under this new leadership, with Medina as the capital city. After the death of Abu Bakr, the next three caliphs were assassinated in power struggles.

In 661, Muawiyah became caliph and created the **Umayyad dynasty**. The Umayyads continued to expand Arab rule, but problems quickly developed. Many believed that the Umayyads were corrupt. Muhammad's grandson, Hussein, led a revolt against them. Hussein was soon killed in battle by the Umayyads, but his rebellion split Islam into two groups—the **Sunni** (loyal to the Umayyads) and the **Shiite** (loyal to Hussein). This split remains in the Muslim world today.

Many Arabs continued to be dissatisfied with Umayyad rule. Abu al-Abbas overthrew the Umayyads in 750 and created the **Abbasid dynasty**, which ruled from Baghdad until about 1258, when the city was sacked by invading Mongols.

Map 1 on page 39 shows the Arabian Peninsula before the spread of Islam. Map 2 on page 41 illustrates the spread of Islam and the Islamic empire. Use both maps to answer the following questions.

1. Name the cities shown on the map through which the Silk Road passed.
   Alexandria, Medina, Mecca, Aden

2. Use the compass rose to describe which portion of the Arabian Peninsula was under Muslim rule during the time of Muhammad. Which body of water provided the empire's western border?
   Under Muhammad, the empire comprised the southwestern part of the peninsula and a small tip in the southeast. The Red Sea provided the western border.

40

Answer Key

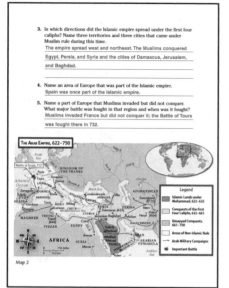

41

3. In which directions did the Islamic empire spread under the first four caliphs? Name three territories and three cities that came under Muslim rule during this time.
The empire spread west and northeast. The Muslims conquered Egypt, Persia, and Syria and the cities of Damascus, Jerusalem, and Baghdad.

4. Name an area of Europe that was part of the Islamic empire.
Spain was once part of the Islamic empire.

5. Name a part of Europe that Muslims invaded but did not conquer. What major battle was fought in that region and when was it fought?
Muslims invaded France but did not conquer it; the Battle of Tours was fought there in 732.

THE ARAB EMPIRE, 622–750

Map 2

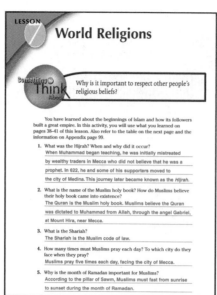

42

LESSON 7

World Religions

Something to Think About

Why is it important to respect other people's religious beliefs?

You have learned about the beginnings of Islam and how its followers built a great empire. In this activity, you will use what you learned on pages 38–41 of this lesson. Also refer to the table on the next page and the information on Appendix page 99.

1. What was the Hijrah? When and why did it occur?
When Muhammad began teaching, he was initially mistreated by wealthy traders in Mecca who did not believe that he was a prophet. In 622, he and some of his supporters moved to the city of Medina. This journey later became known as the *Hijrah*.

2. What is the name of the Muslim holy book? How do Muslims believe their holy book came into existence? Muslims believe the Quran was dictated to Muhammad from Allah, through the angel Gabriel, at Mount Hira, near Mecca.

3. What is the Shariah?
The Shariah is the Muslim code of law.

4. How many times must Muslims pray each day? To which city do they face when they pray?
Muslims pray five times each day, facing the city of Mecca.

5. Why is the month of Ramadan important for Muslims?
According to the pillar of Sawm, Muslims must fast from sunrise to sunset during the month of Ramadan.

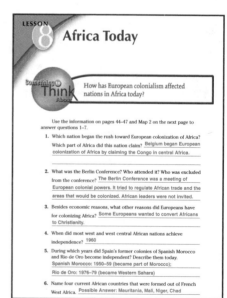

43

6. One of the Five Pillars of Islam is Zakat. Describe the practice of Zakat.
Muslims are to give 2.5 percent of their income to the poor.

7. Rank the major world religions shown in the Appendix in order, from the most to the fewest number of believers.
Christianity, Islam, Hinduism, Buddhism, Judaism

8. Use the information in the Appendix to describe one way Islam is similar to another of the major world religions. Then find one way Islam is different from another religion.
Possible answer: Both Islam and Judaism teach one god; Islam believes in an afterlife of paradise or hell, while Hinduism teaches reincarnation.

9. Three of the major world religions described in the Appendix have their origins in the same part of the world. Name them and explain where they originated. Which is the oldest? Which is the youngest?
Judaism, Christianity, and Islam all originated in the Middle East. Judaism is the oldest; Islam is the youngest.

10. Use the information on Appendix page 99 and your own library research to write three paragraphs on the story of the beginnings of one of the following religions: Christianity, Hinduism, Judaism. You may also choose a different religion if you wish. Write your answer on a separate piece of paper.

The Five Pillars of Islam	
Shahadah	Asserting that Allah is the only God and Muhammad is his prophet.
Salat	Performing set prayers in the direction of Mecca five times a day at specific times. Muslims must take specific postures for the prayers, which are in Arabic.
Sawm	Fasting each day during the month of Ramadan, which is the ninth month of the lunar calendar. During Ramadan, Muslims must not eat or drink between sunrise and sunset. They may eat and drink during the night, however.
Zakat	Giving 2.5 percent of one's income as alms to the poor.
Hajj	Making a pilgrimage to Mecca at least once during one's lifetime, if physically able.

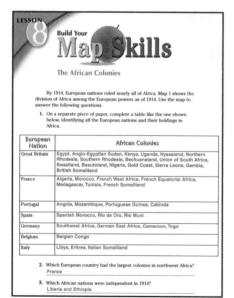

46

LESSON 8

Build Your
Map Skills

The African Colonies

By 1914, European nations ruled nearly all of Africa. Map 1 shows the division of Africa among the European powers as of 1914. Use the map to answer the following questions.

1. On a separate piece of paper, complete a table like the one shown below, identifying all the European nations and their holdings in Africa.

European Nation	African Colonies
Great Britain	Egypt, Anglo-Egyptian Sudan, Kenya, Uganda, Nyasaland, Northern Rhodesia, Southern Rhodesia, Bechuanaland, Union of South Africa, Swaziland, Basutoland, Nigeria, Gold Coast, Sierra Leone, Gambia, British Somaliland
France	Algeria, Morocco, French West Africa, French Equatorial Africa, Madagascar, Tunisia, French Somaliland
Portugal	Angola, Mozambique, Portuguese Guinea, Cabinda
Spain	Spanish Morocco, Rio de Oro, Rio Muni
Germany	Southwest Africa, German East Africa, Cameroon, Togo
Belgium	Belgian Congo
Italy	Libya, Eritrea, Italian Somaliland

2. Which European country had the largest colonies in northwest Africa?
France

3. Which African nations were independent in 1914?
Liberia and Ethiopia

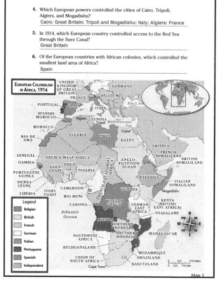

47

4. Which European powers controlled the cities of Cairo, Tripoli, Algiers, and Mogadishu?
Cairo: Great Britain; Tripoli and Mogadishu: Italy; Algiers: France

5. In 1914, which European country controlled access to the Red Sea through the Suez Canal?
Great Britain

6. Of the European countries with African colonies, which controlled the smallest land area of Africa?
Spain

EUROPEAN COLONIALISM IN AFRICA, 1914

Map 1

LESSON 8

Africa Today

Something to Think About

How has European colonialism affected nations in Africa today?

Use the information on pages 44–47 and Map 2 on the next page to answer questions 1–7.

1. Which nation began the rush toward European colonization of Africa? Which part of Africa did this nation claim? Belgium began European colonization of Africa by claiming the Congo in central Africa.

2. What was the Berlin Conference? Who attended it? Who was excluded from the conference? The Berlin Conference was a meeting of European colonial powers. It tried to regulate African trade and the areas that would be colonized. African leaders were not invited.

3. Besides economic reasons, what other reasons did Europeans have for colonizing Africa? Some Europeans wanted to convert Africans to Christianity.

4. When did most west and west central African nations achieve independence? 1960

5. During which years did Spain's former colonies of Spanish Morocco and Rio de Oro become independent? Describe them today.
Spanish Morocco: 1950–59 (became part of Morocco); Rio de Oro: 1976–79 (became Western Sahara)

6. Name four current African countries that were formed out of French West Africa. Possible Answer: Mauritania, Mali, Niger, Chad

48

Answer Key

Answer Key

---

7. What are the two newest independent African nations?
Namibia and Eritrea

Questions 8 and 9 will require library research.

8. Find out the former names of Kinshasa and Kisangani in the Democratic Republic of the Congo. Why do you think the people in the Congo changed these city names after they achieved independence?
Kinshasa: Leopoldville; Kisangani: Stanleyville. These names were changed because they had been named after European colonizers.

9. Select an African nation that has become independent since 1960. On a separate piece of paper, describe how and when the nation became independent, the country's main leaders, main economic activities, and any problems the nation has faced since becoming independent.

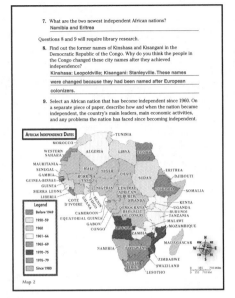

49

Build Your Map Skills

The Incan Empire

Incan society began at Cuzco in the Andes Mountains of Peru in South America. From their capital city, the Incas built an empire that included millions of people and extended from modern-day Ecuador to Chile. Pachacuti Inca, Topa Inca, and Huayna Capac were the rulers who acquired most of the lands of the empire.

Within the empire, conquered tribes ruled themselves through a council of elders. However, all those in the empire were closely controlled by the rigid Incan social rules. Conquered people were generally treated well if they supported and fought for the Incan rulers. They paid a tax of their labor to the Incas, who used it to build an extensive network of roads as well as large forts made of massive stone slabs.

The Incan language was Quechua. The Incas had no writing system; however, they used a system of knotted strings, called **quipu**, for recordkeeping.

The map on the next page shows the expansion of the Incan empire just before the arrival of Pizarro in 1531. Refer to the map and answer the following questions.

1. What was the capital city of the Incan empire? In which present-day country was it located?
Cuzco; Peru

2. At its greatest extent, the Incan empire included parts of which present-day countries? Which ruler expanded the empire the most?
Colombia, Ecuador, Peru, Bolivia, Chile, Argentina; Topa Inca

3. Which river served as the southern limit of the empire?
the Maule River

52

---

4. Describe how Huayna Capac extended the Incan empire.
He expanded the empire north beyond the Guáitara River into Columbia, east further into Ecuador and Peru along the Andes Mountains, and also through western Ecuador to the Pacific Ocean.

5. Identify three cities connected by a road built by the Incas.
Possible answer: Tumbes, Chancay, Nazca

6. What is the highest mountain on the map? How high is it?
Mt. Llullaillaco; 22,057 feet

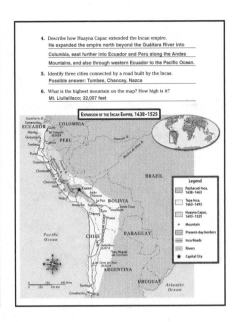

53

Spanish Explorers of the Americas

Something to Think About

How does Spanish culture influence America today?

In this lesson, you learned about some Native American empires and Spanish conquistadors. In this exercise, you will learn more about the Spanish explorers of the Americas. Use the material on pages 50–53 to answer questions 1–5. Question 6 will require additional research.

1. Which European countries were the first rivals for control of the Americas?
Spain and Portugal

2. How did these countries resolve their territorial disputes?
They drew an imaginary boundary line based on the Treaty of Tordesillas (1494), which split the world into two zones. Lands to the east of the line belonged to Portugal, and lands to the west of it belonged to Spain.

3. In general, which parts of the New World did Portugal and Spain eventually claim?
Portugal claimed only Brazil; Spain claimed the Caribbean, Central America, and large portions of North and South America.

4. Which Spanish explorers claimed the most territory for their homeland? Which native empires did they conquer?
Cortés and Pizarro claimed the most territory. Cortés conquered the Aztec empire. Pizarro conquered the Incan empire.

54

---

5. Name a disease that the Spanish explorers brought with them from Europe that devastated the native peoples of the New World.
smallpox

6. You have learned about the explorers Cortés and Pizarro. Now select one of the other explorers shown on the map on page 51 and do some library research following these guidelines:

On a separate piece of paper, draw a detailed map of the route your explorer took to the New World and back. Include destination points, landforms and water forms encountered, cities visited (if any), and lands claimed for Spain. You can also note significant dates or events on the map. Be sure to create a map legend and compass rose.

Write a biography about your explorer in the space below. Include some facts about his early life, travels, and discoveries. Describe how the explorer treated Native Americans and how he is remembered today.

Answers will vary.

55

Build Your Map Skills

The Big Ditch

The Panama Canal opened on August 15, 1914. It is considered to be one of the greatest engineering projects in history. A treaty with Panama gave the United States control of a corridor of land on either side of the canal. The United States owned and operated the canal for about 85 years.

In the 1960s, Panamanians protested the presence of the United States in their country. The canal created many economic benefits for the Panamanians, but many considered the U.S. presence to be colonialism. So, in 1977, U.S. president Jimmy Carter signed a treaty with Panama to give Panama the canal by the year 2000. Today, the canal belongs to the government of Panama.

About 35 to 40 ships pass through the canal each day. The canal is almost 50 miles long, and it takes a ship 8 to 10 hours to pass through it. Locks raise the ships to the level of Gatun Lake. The ships cross the lake and are then lowered again by the locks to sea level. The locks are fed by water from Gatun Lake and Lake Alajuela (Madden Lake). Maintaining the water level in these lakes is essential to the operation of the canal.

Today, almost 100 years after its construction, the canal is still very important to the economy and national defense of the United States. It is also the pride of Panama.

Refer to the map and answer the following questions.

1. Suppose a ship is traveling from the Caribbean Sea to the Bay of Panama. In which direction would the ship be traveling? Name three locks the ship would pass through.
The ship would be traveling southeast. It would go through the Gatun, Pedro Miguel, and Miraflores locks.

2. Name three defense areas (forts) in the canal area. Why do you think they are there?
Possible answer: Fort Davies, Fort Kobbe, and Fort Clayton. They are there to protect the vital shipping lanes of the canal.

58

Answer Key

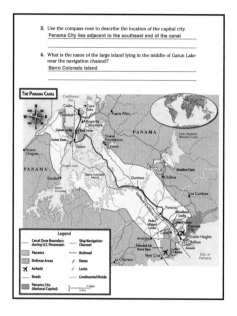

3. Use the compass rose to describe the location of the capital city.
Panama City lies adjacent to the southeast end of the canal

4. What is the name of the large island lying in the middle of Gatun Lake near the navigation channel?
Barro Colorado Island

59

Who Should Own the Canal?

Something to Think About
How have the actions of the United States affected Latin America?

In this lesson, you have learned about the history of the Panama Canal. In this activity, you will think about some issues surrounding ownership of the canal. Use the material on pages 56–59 to answer questions 1–7. Question 8 will require additional research.

1. What is an isthmus?
a narrow bridge of land linking two larger land masses

2. Who first tried to build the Panama Canal? Did they succeed? Why or why not?
The French, under the supervision of Ferdinand de Lesseps, first tried to build the canal. They were unsuccessful. They had underestimated the scope of the job and the difficult terrain.

3. What were two diseases that killed the canal workers?
yellow fever and malaria

4. Which U.S. president was most responsible for the canal?
Theodore Roosevelt

5. What country owned the region surrounding the canal before the United States helped Panama achieve independence?
Colombia

6. What U.S. president signed the treaty to give the canal back to Panama? In which year did Panama get ownership of the canal zone?
Jimmy Carter; 2000

60

---

7. What was happening in Africa at about the time the Panama Canal was being built? (Reread Lesson 8 on pages 44–49 to refresh your memory.) Do you see any similarities between what European countries were doing in Africa and what the United States was doing in Panama? Explain.
Answers will vary.

8. You will now take on the role of an assistant to a U.S. senator in the 1970s. You have been assigned to research the arguments for and against returning the canal to Panama. Use the library to learn as much as you can about the issue. Then, write at least one paragraph in favor of the idea and one paragraph against it. Be sure to cite your reasons.

As you conduct your research and form your arguments, think of the following questions:

• Which cultures and governments were affected the most by the building of the canal? How?

• Did the United States gain the land surrounding the canal in a fair and ethical way? Why or why not?

• Who worked on the canal? What dangers did they face?

• How did the Panama Canal Treaty of 1903 affect U.S.-Panama relations? How did it affect U.S. relations with other Central American nations?

• What effect did the building of the Canal have on a U.S. presence in Central America?

• Who prospered as a result of the Panama Canal?
Answers will vary.

61

Build Your Map Skills

The Invasion at Normandy

The Allied invasion of France took place on June 6, 1944. There were five separate beachheads, or landing areas. They were code-named *Utah, Omaha, Gold, Juno,* and *Sword.* Before the landing, airborne troops, called *paratroopers,* parachuted from airplanes behind enemy lines to secure bridges and other important sites to prepare for the invasion. Also, gliders containing additional troops landed behind enemy lines.

The invasion planners knew they needed a full moon for the invasion to be a success because this would produce a favorable **ocean tide,** or sea depth, at the landing location. The full moon would also provide light for the troops in the early morning hours.

Troops faced a variety of German beach defenses. They included concrete pillboxes for German troops with machine guns and antitank weapons. The beaches and ocean were mined with various devices that would explode when touched.

The landing was very difficult, and there were many casualties (killed and wounded soldiers). However, the invasion was successful because of the determination of the Allies. By June 11, over 300,000 troops, 50,000 vehicles, and 100,000 tons of supplies had landed on the beaches. In about a month, the Allies had established a firm foothold in Normandy.

Map 2 illustrates the Allied invasion at Normandy. Refer to the map to answer the following questions.

1. Which body of water did Allied troops cross during the Normandy invasion?
the English Channel

2. At which beachheads did American troops land? At which beachheads did British and Canadian troops land?
American: Utah and Omaha; British/Canadian: Gold, Juno, and Sword

64

---

3. Which American and British Airborne divisions made landings at Normandy? Near which beachheads did each land?
U.S. 82nd and 101st Airborne landed near Utah beach; the British 6th landed near Sword beach.

4. Which French towns were heavily fortified by the Germans with mine fields?
Cherbourg and Le Havre

5. In which direction is Paris, France, from the beaches at Normandy?
southeast

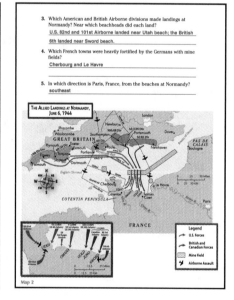

THE ALLIED LANDINGS AT NORMANDY, JUNE 6, 1944

Map 2

65

World War II: The European Theatre

Something to Think About
Why is it important to understand the events that occur during war?

In this lesson, you learned about the invasion at Normandy during World War II. In this activity, you will strengthen your understanding of this key battle as well as other important events during the war. Refer to pages 62–65 to answer questions 1–6. Questions 7 and 8 will require research.

1. Where did the Germans believe that the D-Day landing would take place? Why did they think it would take place there? Where was this location in relation to Normandy beach?
The Germans expected the D-Day landing would be at Pas de Calais, which was northeast of the actual site at Normandy. The Germans expected the invasion there because it was the shortest point across the English Channel, and it had excellent landing beaches.

2. Who was the chief commander of the Normandy invasion? The Allied troops came mainly from which nations?
U.S. general Dwight Eisenhower commanded the Normandy invasion. Allied troops consisted mainly of Britain, Canada, and U.S. forces.

3. About how many Allied troops landed on the beach during the first five days after the invasion at Normandy?
300,000

4. After the Normandy invasion, in which general direction did most Allied troops turn and advance through France?
north and east

5. When did Allied troops cross the Rhine River at Remagen?
March, 1945

66

Answer Key

Panel (page 67):

6. When did Allied invasion forces from southern France and Italy cross into Germany?
December, 1944

7. Use the timeline on page 100 of the Appendix to place the following events in chronological order. Write a "1" in the space beside the first event; write a "2" beside the second event, and so on.

8 Winston Churchill becomes new Prime Minister of Britain.
18 Paris is liberated.
16 Allies land on Italian mainland.
6 Munich Agreement sacrifices Czechoslovakia to Hitler.
5 German troops annex Austria.
11 Germany invades Soviet Union.
7 Germany invades and conquers Poland.
2 Adolf Hitler becomes new Chancellor of Germany.
15 Allies invade Sicily.
9 France surrenders to Germany.
12 Germany and Italy declare war on United States.
19 Allies defeat Germans at the Battle of the Bulge.
14 Battle of Stalingrad.
3 Ethiopia surrenders to Italian forces.
10 Battle of Britain (German air raids on British Isles).
1 Mussolini comes to power in Italy.
20 Germany surrenders to the Allies.
13 British defeat Germans at El Alamein.
4 Italy and Germany form Rome-Berlin Axis.
17 Allies invade Normandy.

8. Select one of the events from question 7 and do some library research to learn more about it. Write at least three paragraphs about the event on a separate piece of paper. Explain what happened, why it happened, and why it was important.

67

Panel (page 70):

LESSON 12

Build Your Map Skills

The Commonwealth of Independent States

After the collapse of the Soviet Union, an alliance of former Soviet republics, named the *Commonwealth of Independent States* (CIS), was founded on December 8, 1991. Members included Belarus, Ukraine, Russia, Armenia, Azerbaijan, Kazakhstan, Kyrgyzstan, Moldova, Tajikistan, Turkmenistan, and Uzbekistan. Georgia joined in 1993. (The former Soviet republics of Estonia, Latvia, and Lithuania declined to join the commonwealth.) The headquarters of the CIS is in Minsk, Belarus.

Members of the CIS operate as independent nations. The CIS is an economic union intended to help encourage and regulate trade. It also attempts to deal with security issues, finance, and law. Though members are independent, the CIS has been criticized by some as simply a way for Russia to maintain some measure of control over former regions of the Soviet Union.

The future of the CIS has been questioned by some member states. For example, Georgia has made gestures toward NATO and withdrew from the Council of Defense Ministers in 2006. Ukraine is considering halting its financial contributions to CIS. In addition, Turkmenistan reduced its status to an associate member in 2005.

Map 2 shows the nations that were formed from the breakup of the Soviet Union. Use the map to answer the following questions.

1. Which former Soviet republics have never been members of the CIS? Name one thing these nations have in common geographically.
Estonia, Latvia, and Lithuania have never been members of the CIS. They are all Baltic Sea states.

2. After Russia, what is the largest nation in the CIS?
Kazakhstan

70

Panel (page 71):

3. Which CIS members probably profit the most from trade through the Black Sea? How do you know?
Ukraine, Russia, and Georgia probably profit the most from Black Sea trade because these nations border the Black Sea.

4. Which four CIS members share a border with China?
Russia, Kazakhstan, Kyrgyzstan, Tajikistan

5. Which three CIS members lie closest to Europe?
Belarus, Ukraine, and Moldova

6. Which CIS nations are landlocked (that is, have no access to an ocean)? (Note that the Aral and Caspian seas do not provide ocean access.)
Moldova, Belarus, Armenia, Kyrgyzstan, Tajikistan, Uzbekistan, Azerbaijan, Turkmenistan, Kazakhstan

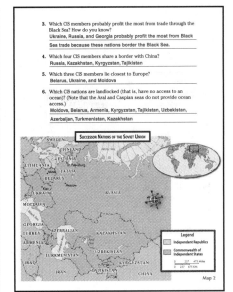

Map 2

71

Panel (page 72):

LESSON 12

Struggles in the Soviet Satellite States

Something to Think About
How have the struggles of the Soviet satellite states affected American history?

In this activity, you will learn more about freedom movements in Eastern Europe and the current status of the former Soviet republics. Use the material on pages 68–71 and Appendix page 101 to answer questions 1–7. Questions 8–9 will require additional research.

1. Who were the main rivals in the Cold War?
the Soviet Union and the United States/Western Europe

2. What is NATO? Why was it formed? What organization did the Soviet Union and its allies form in response to NATO?
To protect their interests, the United States and some Western European nations formed the North Atlantic Treaty Organization (NATO) for mutual defense. In response, the Soviet Union formed the Warsaw Pact in 1955.

3. Name one Western European nation that did not belong to NATO. Name one Eastern European nation that did not belong to the Warsaw Pact.
Possible answer: Switzerland (west) and Yugoslavia (east)

4. What was the Brezhnev Doctrine?
Under this doctrine, the Soviets used military force to put down dissident movements that challenged Communist authority.

5. Name one consequence of the Soviet style of government.
Possible answer: Government control of the economy discouraged hard work and efficiency.

72

Panel (page 73):

6. What was perestroika? Perestroika began under whose leadership? What did it bring about?
Mikhail Gorbachev began perestroika (restructuring) to change the Soviet economic system to a market economy. It led to political reform that allowed political parties other than the Communist Party and ultimately broke up the Soviet Union.

7. Which was the first Soviet republic to declare its independence? Besides Russia itself, which was the last?
Lithuania was the first; Ukraine was the last.

Do some library research to answer the following questions.

8. Before the breakup of the Soviet Union, the Soviets put down challenges to Communist authority in their satellite states. Select one of the following dissident movements and write three paragraphs about it on a separate piece of paper. In your paper, discuss what happened, when and where it happened, why it happened, who the principal leaders were, and how it turned out.

| East German Uprising of 1953 | Prague Spring (1968) |
| Hungarian Revolution (1956) | Polish Solidarity movement (1980s) |

9. Select one of the countries that formed after the breakup of the Soviet Union (see the list on Appendix page 101). Find the following information for that country. If necessary, record your answers on a separate piece of paper. (For "Ethnic tensions or international disputes," note any ethnic tension within the country or problems the country is having with other nations.)

• Country:
• Date of Independence:
• Natural resources:
• Main imports and exports:
• Primary ethnic groups:
• Ethnic tensions or international disputes:

73

Panel (page 76):

LESSON 13

Build Your Map Skills

Ecoregions on a World Map

Different plants grow in different ecoregions. For example, deciduous trees typically grow in temperate, mid-latitude ecoregions that do not experience wide temperature changes. **Deciduous trees** produce leaves, which they usually drop every fall. Northern ecoregions support more **coniferous trees**, which produce needles rather than leaves. Map 1 illustrates and describes the different ecoregions of the world. Use the map to answer the questions. Also refer to Appendix page 102.

1. Which areas of the world have tropical rainforests?
Tropical rainforests are located in north-central South America, parts of central and west-central Africa, southeast Asia, and the island chains of the South Pacific.

2. Which ecoregion predominates in Europe? Where can this ecoregion be found in North America?
The temperate broadleaf forest ecoregion predominates in Europe. It can be found in the eastern half of the United States.

3. Which two continents have the most desert in proportion to their total land area?
Africa and Australia

4. Which ecoregions occupy most of the lands north of 60° N latitude?
boreal forest/taiga, tundra, and polar/mountains

5. Describe one difference between most trees growing in the eastern part of the United States and those that grow in Canada.
Trees in the eastern United States are mostly deciduous trees that lose their leaves each fall; trees in Canada are mostly coniferous trees that stay green year-round.

76

Answer Key

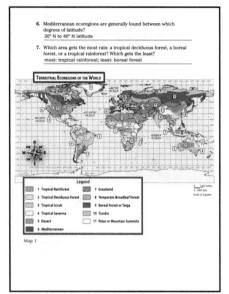

6. Mediterranean ecoregions are generally found between which degrees of latitude?
   30° N to 40° N latitude

7. Which area gets the most rain: a tropical deciduous forest, a boreal forest, or a tropical rainforest? Which gets the least?
   most: tropical rainforest; least: boreal forest

Map 1

77

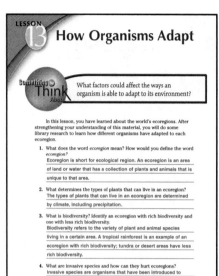

LESSON 13
How Organisms Adapt

Something to Think About
What factors could affect the ways an organism is able to adapt to its environment?

In this lesson, you have learned about the world's ecoregions. After strengthening your understanding of this material, you will do some library research to learn how different organisms have adapted to each ecoregion.

1. What does the word *ecoregion* mean? How would you define the word *ecoregion*?
   Ecoregion is short for ecological region. An ecoregion is an area of land or water that has a collection of plants and animals that is unique to that area.

2. What determines the types of plants that can live in an ecoregion?
   The types of plants that can live in an ecoregion are determined by climate, including precipitation.

3. What is biodiversity? Identify an ecoregion with rich biodiversity and one with less biodiversity.
   Biodiversity refers to the variety of plant and animal species living in a certain area. A tropical rainforest is an example of an ecoregion with rich biodiversity; tundra or desert areas have less rich biodiversity.

4. What are invasive species and how can they hurt ecoregions?
   Invasive species are organisms that have been introduced to an area where they do not occur naturally. They may eventually displace or destroy an ecoregion's native organisms.

78

5. Name one way rainfall in a tropical deciduous forest differs from rainfall in a temperate broadleaf forest.
   In a tropical deciduous forest, rainy and dry seasons are distinct; in a temperate broadleaf forest, rainfall is more evenly distributed throughout the year.

6. Name a difference between tropical savanna and grassland ecoregions.
   A tropical savanna contains more trees than a grassland.

7. Name one ecoregion that does not support trees of any kind.
   Possible answer: polar or mountain summits

8. Now do some library research to complete the following table. Find a plant or animal that lives in each ecoregion. Describe one way the organism has adapted to its environment. Answers will vary.

Ecoregion	Organism	Adaptation to Environment
Tropical Rainforest		
Tropical Deciduous Forest		
Tropical Scrub		
Tropical Savanna		
Desert		
Mediterranean		
Grassland		
Temperate Broadleaf Forest		
Boreal Forest/Taiga		
Tundra		
Polar or Mountain Summits		

79

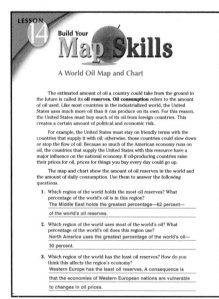

LESSON 14
Build Your
Map Skills

A World Oil Map and Chart

The estimated amount of oil a country could take from the ground in the future is called its **oil reserves. Oil consumption** refers to the amount of oil used. Like most countries in the industrialized world, the United States uses much more oil than it can produce on its own. For this reason, the United States must buy much of its oil from foreign countries. This creates a certain amount of political and economic risk.

For example, the United States must stay on friendly terms with the countries that supply it with oil; otherwise, those countries could slow down or stop the flow of oil. Because so much of the American economy runs on oil, the countries that supply the United States with this resource have a major influence on the national economy. If oil-producing countries raise their prices for oil, prices for things you buy every day could go up.

The map and chart show the amount of oil reserves in the world and the amount of daily consumption. Use them to answer the following questions.

1. Which region of the world holds the most oil reserves? What percentage of the world's oil is in this region?
   The Middle East holds the greatest percentage—62 percent—of the world's oil reserves.

2. Which region of the world uses most of the world's oil? What percentage of the world's oil does this region use?
   North America uses the greatest percentage of the world's oil—30 percent.

3. Which region of the world has the least oil reserves? How do you think this affects the region's economy?
   Western Europe has the least reserves. A consequence is that the economies of Western European nations are vulnerable to changes in oil prices.

82

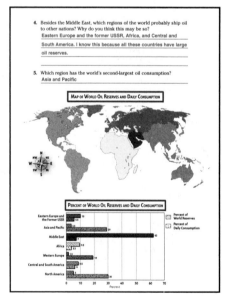

4. Besides the Middle East, which regions of the world probably ship oil to other nations? Why do you think this may be so?
   Eastern Europe and the former USSR, Africa, and Central and South America. I know this because all these countries have large oil reserves.

5. Which region has the world's second-largest oil consumption?
   Asia and Pacific

Map of World Oil Reserves and Daily Consumption

Percent of World Oil Reserves and Daily Consumption

83

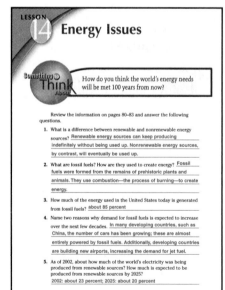

LESSON 14
Energy Issues

Something to Think About
How do you think the world's energy needs will be met 100 years from now?

Review the information on pages 80–83 and answer the following questions.

1. What is a difference between renewable and nonrenewable energy sources? Renewable energy sources can keep producing indefinitely without being used up. Nonrenewable energy sources, by contrast, will eventually be used up.

2. What are fossil fuels? How are they used to create energy? Fossil fuels were formed from the remains of prehistoric plants and animals. They use combustion—the process of burning—to create energy.

3. How much of the energy used in the United States today is generated from fossil fuels? about 85 percent

4. Name two reasons why demand for fossil fuels is expected to increase over the next few decades. In many developing countries, such as China, the number of cars has been growing; these are almost entirely powered by fossil fuels. Additionally, developing countries are building new airports, increasing the demand for jet fuel.

5. As of 2002, about how much of the world's electricity was being produced from renewable sources? How much is expected to be produced from renewable sources by 2025?
   2002: about 23 percent; 2025: about 20 percent

84

Answer Key

Perform your own library research to answer the questions below.

6. At current rates of consumption, how long is the world's reserve of oil expected to last? How long will reserves of natural gas last?
Answers will vary depending on sources. Possible answer: At current consumption levels, remaining oil reserves will last about 45 years; gas reserves will last about 65 years.

7. Think about what you have learned about fossil fuels in this lesson. Then, describe one scientific and one political reason why the United States should consider developing renewable energy technologies.
Scientific reason: to reduce pollution; political reason: U.S. relations with other countries might change for the better.

8. Complete the table below about some of the renewable sources of energy. Briefly describe how each type of energy works and list some advantages and disadvantages of each. After you have filled in the information below, write one paragraph, on a separate piece of paper, describing which source of renewable energy has the best chance of being used widely throughout the United States and why.

Renewable Energy Source	How Does It Work?	Advantages	Disadvantages
Wind Power	Wind turns a turbine's blades, which spin a shaft connected to a generator that makes electricity.	Renewable, clean fuel source; produces no air pollution; low cost; creates income for rural land owners.	Large up-front investment; wind may be inconsistent; good wind sites are often far from cities; objection to noise of rotors and overall appearance.
Hydropower	Factories capture flowing water and move it through turbines to create electricity.	Renewable, clean fuel source; produces no air pollution.	May limit the passage of migrating fish; lower water quality; alter stream levels; change natural habitat; and undependable in times of drought.
Solar Power	Panels use mirrors to capture the sun's heat to run conventional generators that create electricity.	Renewable, clean fuel source; produces no air pollution; low cost.	More practical in southern states than in northern climates.

85

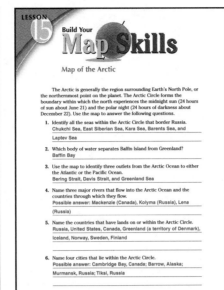

LESSON 15

Build Your Map Skills

Map of the Arctic

The Arctic is generally the region surrounding Earth's North Pole, or the northernmost point on the planet. The Arctic Circle forms the boundary within which the north experiences the midnight sun (24 hours of sun about June 21) and the polar night (24 hours of darkness about December 22). Use the map to answer the following questions.

1. Identify all the seas within the Arctic Circle that border Russia.
Chukchi Sea, East Siberian Sea, Kara Sea, Barents Sea, and Laptev Sea

2. Which body of water separates Baffin Island from Greenland?
Baffin Bay

3. Use the map to identify three outlets from the Arctic Ocean to either the Atlantic or the Pacific Ocean.
Bering Strait, Davis Strait, and Greenland Sea

4. Name three major rivers that flow into the Arctic Ocean and the countries through which they flow.
Possible answer: Mackenzie (Canada), Kolyma (Russia), Lena (Russia)

5. Name the countries that have lands on or within the Arctic Circle.
Russia, United States, Canada, Greenland (a territory of Denmark), Iceland, Norway, Sweden, Finland

6. Name four cities that lie within the Arctic Circle.
Possible answer: Cambridge Bay, Canada; Barrow, Alaska; Murmansk, Russia; Tiksi, Russia

88

---

7. The Arctic Circle is the traditional boundary for the Arctic region. Identify one body of water, one city, and one island that are not within the Arctic Circle but which would be considered "Arctic" if the 50 degree Fahrenheit isotherm were used as the boundary line.
Possible answer: Water—Bering Sea; city—Nome, Alaska; island—Aleutian Islands

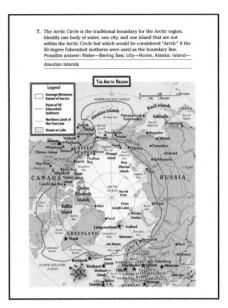

89

LESSON 15

Life in the Arctic

Something to Think About

In what ways might life in the Arctic affect you?

Answer the following questions. Refer to pages 86–89, if necessary.

1. How big is the Arctic region compared with the United States?
It is about 1.5 times the size of the United States

2. How long each year is the Arctic covered with ice? How much melts during the summer?
The Arctic is covered with ice about nine months per year. About half of that ice melts in the summer months.

3. What is the tree line?
The tree line is the point north of which trees no longer grow.

4. How has the melting of perennial sea ice changed over the past several decades? How might this impact life in the Arctic?
More of the ice pack is melting in summer. This could impact the Arctic in many ways. For example, polar bears use the ice to reach the sea where they feed. Less ice will make it harder for them to find food.

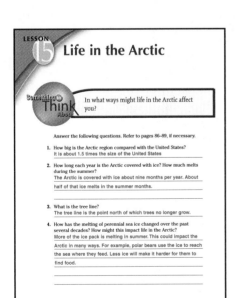

90

---

5. The table briefly describes the three biological communities, or realms, of the Arctic Ocean. The diagram illustrates a **food web** involving some of the organisms of the various realms. The arrows in the diagram indicate that the polar bear feeds on the seal, which feeds on the arctic cod, which feeds on under-ice crustaceans and gelatinous zooplankton.

Do library research to create your own Arctic food-web diagram on a separate sheet of paper. You should use at least one organism from each realm; use more if you like. Label each realm and each organism. Answers will vary.

Name	Description	Examples
Sea-Ice Realm	Includes organisms that live in, on, and just under arctic ice	Diatoms, algae, bacteria, viruses, fungi, polar bears, arctic cod
Pelagic Realm	Includes organisms that live between the ocean surface and the ocean bottom	Zooplankton, fish, squids, seals, whales
Benthic Realm	Includes organisms that live on the ocean bottom	Sponges, bivalves, crustaceans, sea anemones

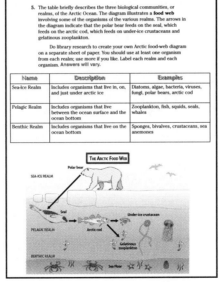

91

Notes